Helion & Company Limited
Unit 8 Amherst Business Centre
Budbrooke Road
Warwick
CV34 5WE
England
Tel. 01926 499 619
Email: info@helion.co.uk
Website: www.helion.co.uk
Twitter: @helionbooks
Visit our blog http://blog.helion.co.uk/

Designed and typeset by Farr out Publications, Wokingham, Berkshire
Cover design by Paul Hewitt, Battlefield Design (www.battlefi eld-design.co.uk)

ISBN 978-1-914059-30-8

British Library Cataloguing-in-Publication Data
A catalogue record for this book is available from the British Library

We always welcome receiving book proposals from prospective authors.

CONTENTS

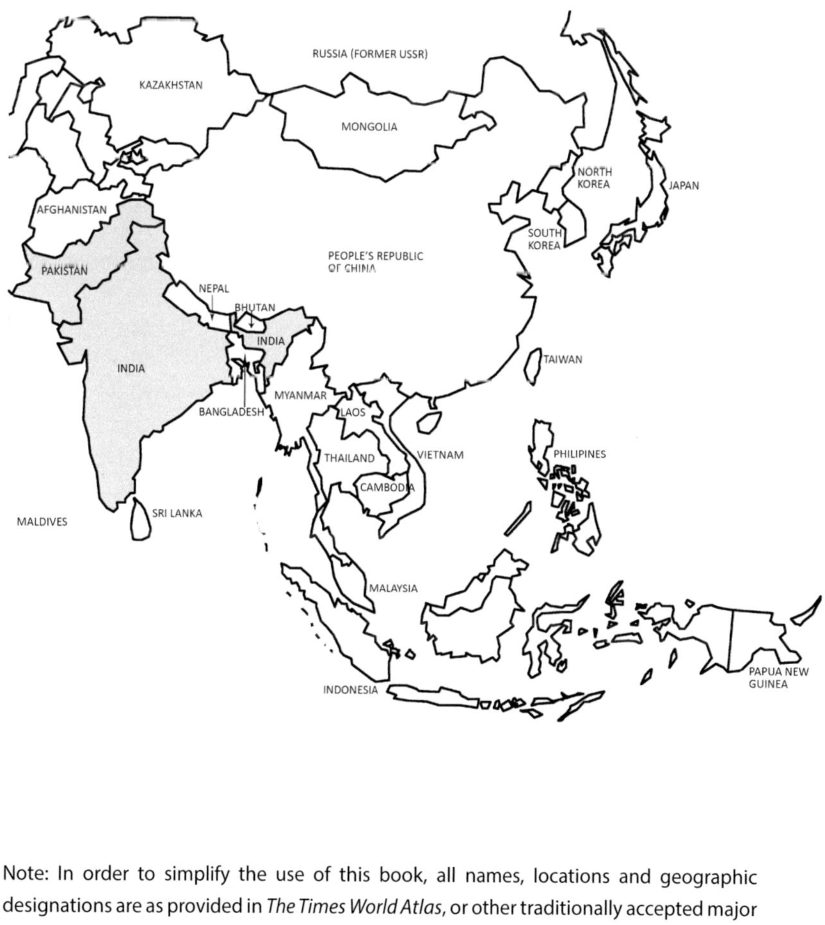

Note: In order to simplify the use of this book, all names, locations and geographic designations are as provided in *The Times World Atlas*, or other traditionally accepted major sources of reference, as of the time of described events.

ABBREVIATIONS

AAA	anti-aircraft artillery
AAC	Army Aviation Corps (India)
AAD	Army Air Defence (India)
AB	air base
ADC	Air Defence Command (India)
ADCC	Air Defence Command Centre (India)
ADGES	Air Defence Ground Environment System (India)
AGPL	Actual Ground Position Line
AIDMK	All India Anna Dravida Munnetra Kazhagam (All India Anna Dravidan Progressive Federation)
AM	Air Marshal (military commissioned officer rank, equivalent to lieutenant-general)
An	Antonov (the design bureau led by Oleg Antonov)
APC	armoured personnel carrier
ARC	Aviation Research Centre (India)
ARDE	Armament Research and Development Establishment (India)
ASC	Army Service Corps (India)
ASCC	Air Standardisation Coordinating Committee
ATGM	anti-tank guided missile
BIT	Brigade Intelligence Team
BJP	Bharatiya Janata Party (India)
BSF	Border Security Force (India)
CADA	Corps of Air Defence Artillery (India)
CBM	confidence-building measures
CBRN	chemical, biological, radiological, nuclear
CCRP	continuously controlled release point
CEP	circular error probable
CO	Commanding officer
COIN	counterinsurgency
CRC	Control and Reporting Centre
DGMI	Director General Military Intelligence (India)
DRDO	Defence Research and Development Organization
ELINT	electronic intelligence
EME	Electrical and Mechanical Engineers
FAA	forward assembly area
FF	Frontier Force (Pakistan)
GBP	British Pounds Sterling
GOC	General Officer Commanding
GPS	Global Positioning System
GR	Gurkha Rifles
HAL	Hindustan Aeronautics Limited
HAWS	High Altitude Warfare School (India)
HEER	high explosive extended-range
HMG	heavy machine gun
HU	Helicopter Unit (Indian Air Force)
IAF	Indian Air Force
IB	Intelligence Bureau (India)
IAP	international airport
ICV	infantry combat vehicle
IFV	infantry fighting vehicle
IFG	Indian Field Gun
IFSU	Intelligence and Field Surveillance Unit
INC	Indian National Congress
INSAS	Indian Small Arms System
ISI	Inter-Services Intelligence (Pakistan)
JAK LI	Jamu and Kashmir Light Infantry
JCO	Junior Commissioned Officer
JIC	Joint Intelligence Committee
LAC	Line of Actual Control
LDP	laser designation pod
LFG	Light Field Gun (India)
LGB	laser guided bomb
LoC	Line of Control
LTTE	Liberation Tigers of Tamil Eelam (Sri Lanka)
MANPADs	man-portable air defence system/s
MBB	Messerschmitt-Bölkow-Böhm (Germany)
MBRL	multi-barrel rocket launcher
MBT	main battle tank
MiG	Mikoyan i Gurevich (the design bureau led by Artyom Ivanovich Mikoyan and Mikhail Iosifovich Gurevich, also known as OKB-155 or MMZ 'Zenit')
MI	Military Intelligence (India)
MMG	medium machine gun (FN MAG on a tripod mount)
MOF	Mobile Observation Flight
MOP	Mobile Observation Post
NLI	Northern Light Infantry (Pakistan)
OC	Officer in Command
OCU	Operational Conversion Unit
OTU	Operational Training Unit
PAF	Pakistan Air Force
Para SF	Paratroop Regiment (Special Forces [Capable])
PML-N	Pakistan Muslim League (Nawaz)
POK	Pakistan Occupied Kashmir
PRC	People's Republic of China (or 'mainland China')
Raj Rif	Rajputana Rifles (India)
RAPID	Reorganized Army Plains Infantry Division (India)
RAF	Royal Air Force (of the United Kingdom)
RAW	Research and Analysis Wing (India)
RR	Rasthtriya Rifles (India)
SAM	surface-to-air missile
SFF	Special Frontier Force (India)
SIGINT	signals intelligence
SLR	Self Loading Rifle
Sqn	Squadron
SSG	Special Services Group (Pakistan)
SU	Signals unit
TRU	transportable radar unit
UAV	unmanned aerial vehicle
WASO	Winter Air Support Operations
WSO	Weapons System Officer

1
INTRODUCTION AND BACKGROUND

The late South Asia expert, Professor Stephen Cohen, once described the Siachen conflict between India and Pakistan as "two bald men fighting over a comb". That analogy has found some currency among elite intellectual circles but it is an utterly nonsensical comparison that belies a lack of appreciation of either geopolitical or strategic reality. In India's strategic and tactical military calculus, the Siachen Glacier and the Saltoro Ridge are lynchpins to its control over Ladakh and the security of its military positions therein. Despite being a desolate and remote battlefield at extreme altitudes, India remains determined to hold its positions, no matter the cost.

In some ways, the title of this book is a bit of a misnomer. The Siachen conflict is not merely about Siachen and the conflict between India and Pakistan over the Glacier and the Saltoro Ridge. It is as much about the reorientation of the northern reaches of the Ladakh region as well as its eastern sectors as a zone of a potential conflict between three nuclear powers – China and Pakistan on one side and India on the other. India has invested more in military resources to maintain its positions in Ladakh, despite the extreme weather, than might be seemingly warranted for its military orientation towards Pakistan, including mountain divisions and a new Strike Corps.

The Glacier

The Siachen Glacier, a bleak and inhospitable place, is a feature situated in the eastern Karakoram Range of the Himalayas ranges at about 35.421226°N and 77.109540°E, just northeast of the point NJ9842, the latter being the point where the Line of Control between India and Pakistan ends.[1] Being some 76 kilometres (47 miles) long, it is the longest glacier in the Karakoram and in the world's non-polar areas, it is the second-longest. The glacier has an altitude of 5,753 metres (18,875 feet) above sea level from its head at Indira Col situated at the India-China border down to 3,620 metres (11,875 feet) at its end.[2]

Since 1984, the entire Siachen Glacier, with all major passes, has been under the administration and control of India (since August 2019 being part of the union territory of Ladakh, located in the Kashmir region).[3] As part of the ongoing dispute over the Kashmir region, Pakistan maintains a territorial claim over the Siachen Glacier and exercises physical control of the region west of Saltoro Ridge, to the west of the glacier, Pakistani military posts are located some 3,000 feet below India's posts, more than 100 of which are located on the glacial ridge.[4]

Geologically, the Siachen Glacier lies immediately south of the great drainage divide that separates the Eurasian Plate of central Asia from the Indian subcontinent in the heavily glaciated portion of the Karakoram which is sometimes known as the 'Third Pole'. The actual glacier lies between the Saltoro Ridge, located on the immediate west, and the main Karakoram Range located to the east.

Also known as the 'Third Pole', the area of the Siachen Glacier is a snow-covered mountain desert, and – because of its importance as a water source – the highest active battlefield in the world. (Indian Army)

The Siachen Glacier is bleak, inhospitable and represents the highest battlefield in the world, where deaths from avalanches, cold induced ailments, high altitude sickness and snow accidents are far more common than deaths in actual combat. However, for India, it has become a vital part of its military interests in the Ladakh region.

The Saltoro Ridge of the Siachen Glacier serves as a geographical divide that prevents a direct geographical link between Pakistani controlled areas of Kashmir and China. Given India's apprehensions of the military nexus between the two countries, it desires to prevent them from developing direct, geographical military linkage in the area. Siachen, in addition, because of its high altitude, enables India to keep effective surveillance of the Gilgit and Baltistan regions of Pakistani controlled Kashmir.[5]

The crest of the Saltoro Ridge ranges from 5,450 metres (17,880 feet) to 7,720 metres (25,330 feet). The major access passes on the Saltoro Ridge are – taking them in a north to south orientation, Sia La at 5,589 metres (18,336 feet), Bilafond La at 5,450 metres (17,880 feet) and Gyong La at 5,689 metres (18,665 feet).[6]

The Siachen Glacier system, inclusive of all its tributary glaciers, is enormous at some 700 square kilometres in area and is the largest ice mass outside of the Polar regions of the planet. In its north, from Indira Col, which is located at an altitude above 5,753 metres (18,875 feet) to the Siachen base camp located along the Shyok River in the Nubra Valley, the Siachen Glacier is some 75 kilometres long and five kilometres wide. The Siachen Glacier is joined by several smaller ones and the point at Indira Col dominates the Shaksgam Valley, ceded by Pakistan to China.[7]

Access to the Siachen Glacier from Jammu, involves the crossing of no fewer than five mountain ranges. Beginning with the Dhaula Dhar and then the Pir Panjal which provide access into the Kashmir Valley and Srinagar, the next stage involves crossing the Great Himalayan Range passing through Zojila and the Zanskar Range which provides access to Leh. From Leh, the route passes through the Ladakh Range and through Khardung La, ending in the Nubra River Valley. The Nubra River flows out of the Siachen Glacier and forms a tributary to the Indus River.[8]

Zojila and Khardung La are open only for short periods of time in the summer, making the scope for moving supplies and reinforcements into the Siachen Glacier very season and time sensitive. The region is snow-covered throughout the year and suffers from extremely low temperatures ranging from -50 degrees Celsius to -70 degrees Celsius. Winds of exceedingly high velocities, low ambient oxygen levels and whiteout conditions where there is no visibility are routine. The conditions cause a variety of diseases among troops stationed on the Siachen Glacier and mountain sickness, hallucinations, frostbite and pulmonary oedema are serious ailments which have resulted in deaths.[9]

The terrain imposes severe limitations on mobility. Troops have to be self-contained and are thus heavily laden during moves, though this is variable. Climate dictates that avalanche-prone areas are crossed early in the mornings when the ice is at its thickest and when the risk of an avalanche is at its lowest. When troops need to move to new locations, lightly-laden troops make a path and then return to their base camp with the heavier loads being transferred across this new path to the new location. This makes movement to new locations very time consuming and requires care in selection.[10]

The logistics-related challenges are nothing short of enormous and will be detailed in later chapters. However, the terrain and environment necessitate the establishment of a base camp which India has done at the 'snout' of the Siachen Glacier to enable the performance of administrative functions as well as to prepare troops through acclimatisation before they can be inducted onto the Siachen Glacier for duties. There are long lines of communications from the Army's maintenance areas in the rear and as such several administrative camps have been established at intervals within marching distance.[11]

It is hard to overstate the logistical and medical challenges facing troops on the Siachen Glacier. It is no exaggeration to say that the entire Indian military capability on the glacier and Saltoro Ridge is dependent on an air bridge with helicopters providing an essential lifeline to the troops on the Siachen Glacier with very light helicopters, each with extremely limited payloads and limited avionics, providing the final part of an air bridge that starts with fixed wing aircraft bringing supplies to Leh and advanced landing grounds for onward transport by medium helicopters to base camps and thereafter to troops.[12]

The Siachen Glacier and the Saltoro Ridge are the highest battlefields on the planet. Though the warring nations have only been involved in sporadic combat, each army wages, by dint of their deployment at extreme altitude and in extraordinarily hostile terrain, a war against the environment on a daily basis. That both countries continue to commit large forces to the theatre with brigade sized formations being assigned on permanent deployment with battalions being rotated through to allow for acclimatisation is a testimony to the perceived importance of the region that both armies continue their deployment.

Importance to India

India's concerns over China's massively enhanced infrastructure in the Aksai Chin area of the Kashmir, which the latter has effectively annexed since 1962, and its ever-assertive territorial claims in

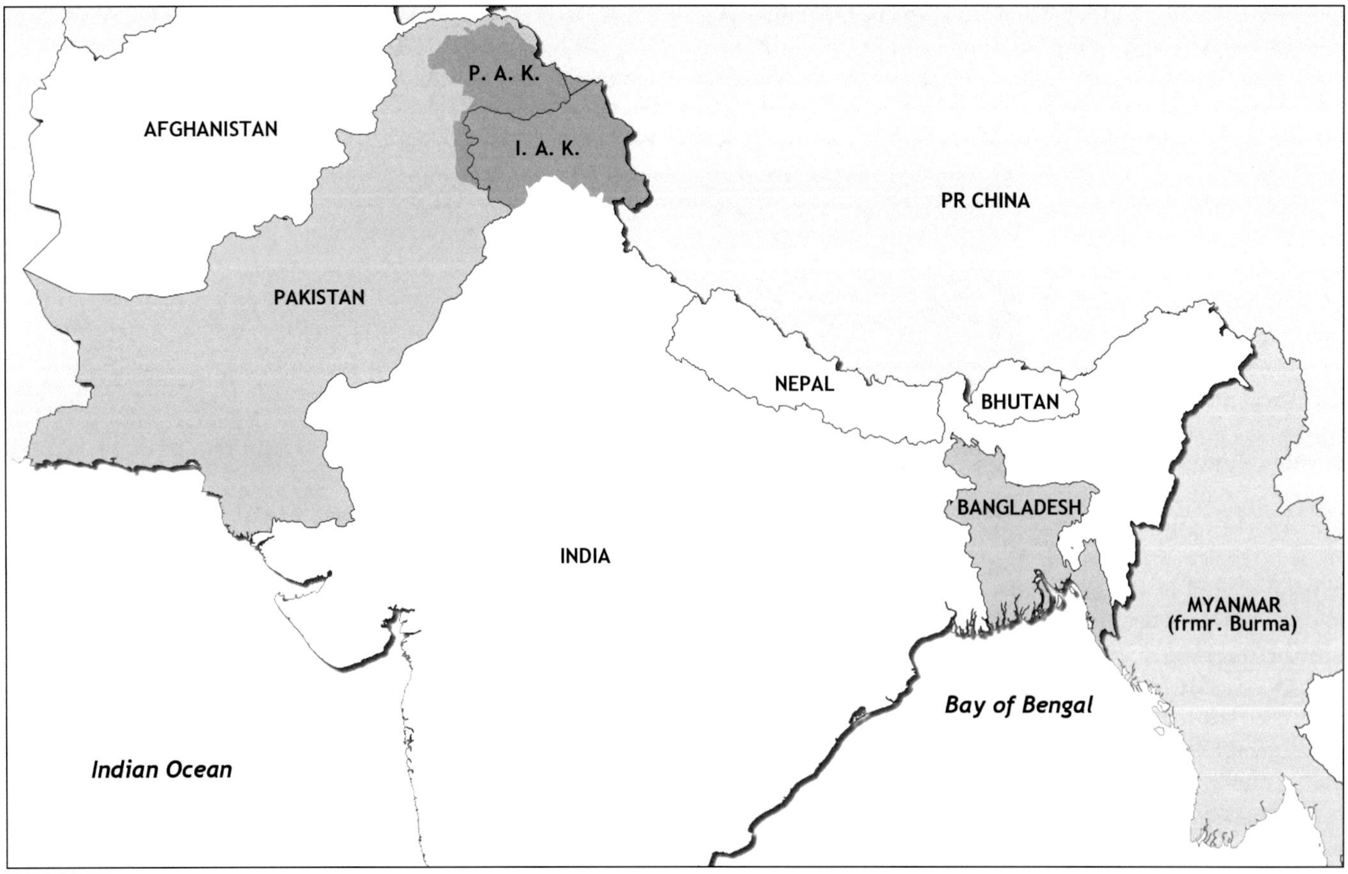

A map of Pakistan and central and northern India, with the Pakistan-Administered Kashmir (P.A.K.) and Indian-Administered Kashmir (I.A.K.) marked in dark grey. (Map by Tom Cooper)

Ladakh, culminating in the clashes of 2020, has meant that India uses its positions in Siachen to pose a threat to the China-Pakistan Karakoram Highway through India's control of the Karakoram Pass. The ability to interdict this crucial artery is perhaps the reason that India has taken such huge risks to seize and thereafter to hold the Siachen Glacier, despite its high costs in money, materiel and manpower. Moreover, India has taken extreme steps to secure its ability to sustain its forces on the Siachen Glacier, to the extent that in 1999, it was prepared to go to war with Pakistan after the latter infiltrated troops in the Kargil region and which posed a potential threat to India's supply lines to Siachen.[13]

The depth of Indian concern of a hostile nexus between China and Pakistan was and is prevalent and, as India's Northern Command would note in 1984:

> With an all-weather Karakoram highway to the west and the Aksai Chin road to the east, Ladakh is open to a pincer by these powers. Pakistani occupation of the Siachen up to the Karakoram Pass would lead to their domination of the Nubra Valley and the route down to Leh. Indian positions in Siachen as well as in the vicinity of the Karakoram Pass are thus a formidable wedge between Pakistan Occupied Kashmir (POK), the 4,500 square kilometres ceded by Pakistan to China and Aksai Chin occupied by China after the 1962 conflict. Pakistani occupation of the region would in a way provide a cushion to the Chinese positions already prevalent in the area.[14]

Thus, the war in Siachen is much more than merely a conflict over the glacier and the Saltoro Ridge. It is part of India's broader concerns about its positions in Ladakh. No analysis of the Siachen conflict can afford to ignore the preparations India has increasingly made for a conflict with China, to the extent of raising specialised formations for that task. The fact that India foresees a China-Pakistan combined operation in Ladakh at least partially explains India's operation to take control of the Siachen Glacier and its complete determination to hold their positions on the glacier and the Saltoro Ridge. This determination has come at great cost both in terms of expenditure and in terms of lives lost or adversely impacted.

Siachen in Context

The Siachen conflict and its attendant complications regarding both India-Pakistan and India-China relations have to be seen in the context of the competing claims, concerns and imperatives within the broader Kashmir region. Pakistan sees Kashmir as being 'unfinished business from partition of 1948' and believes on a philosophical level that the Muslim-majority region should belong to Pakistan. Set against that is India's view that it intends never to allow another geographic split along religious lines and will do whatever is necessary to ensure its territorial integrity, to the extent of combating any attempt at disruption and by whatever means necessary. Into this mix comes China which has never accepted the old pre-Independence border with India and has been steadily trying to use its great political, economic and military muscle to push a geographical settlement on its terms.

India's conflict with Pakistan in Siachen, while closely linked to the Kashmir dispute between India and Pakistan and its attendant religious dimensions, has acquired a life of its own, with India looking at the conflict in much broader geopolitical terms which inevitably baffle some casual observers or those not appreciating the multiplicity of layers that are involved in India's thinking on the issue with both its concerns over Pakistani encroachment in Ladakh, and China's attempts to forge a geographical land-link with Pakistan through the Karakoram Highway – with the risks that brings to India's own military and political positions in the wider regions of Ladakh.

When set against this, India's hold on the Siachen Glacier is intended to enforce both its geographical claims to the territory as well as to prevent a secure physical link between Pakistan and China through which these two countries could act in concert to physically threaten Indian positions not only on the Siachen Glacier but also in other areas of Ladakh and Kashmir. The tensions with China and Pakistan provide India with much incentive to keep its hold in the area as well as to improve and reinforce its ability to supply, sustain and, if need be, expand its presence and military assets in theatre.

The Siachen conflict thus represents a near-continuous confrontation between India and Pakistan ever since 1984. Other conflicts have flared up around them, both internal and external, but the Siachen Glacier and the Saltoro Ridge have remained areas of contention.

Ironically, this conflict is one where the environment is more of an adversary than combat is. It costs both countries heavily in terms of both money and manpower, but the conflict persists, albeit with a ceasefire persisting for a number of years and combat being very infrequent. However, while the conflict has its own dynamics of geography, strategic importance and geopolitics, the India-Pakistan conflict – with China not being forgotten – is broader and has a very troubling past. India and Pakistan have fought four wars – in 1948, 1965, 1971 and 1999 – and all of the conflicts have involved the former princely state of Kashmir and include the territory of Ladakh. Two conflicts – 1965 and 1971 – involved wide scale conflict with combat stretching across the subcontinent and involving land, air and sea forces. Fighting in 1948 and 1999, however, was limited to Kashmir. India and China clashed in 1962 and again in 1987. The tensions resulting from these conflicts cast a shadow over the entire region and directly impacts on the importance of the Siachen Glacier in geopolitical calculations.

2
A HISTORY OF TENSION AND CONFLICT

Siachen is very much part of the historical legacy of colonial rule and the subsequent partition of the Indian subcontinent. However, it is complicated by its hostile geography which made demarcation of both the India-Pakistan border as well as the Line of Control exceedingly difficult. With the countries having a tense history, plagued by wars and distrust, it is not surprising that the importance of Siachen has an importance out of all proportion to its location.

A Bloody Legacy

In 1947, the entity that was British India gained independence, accompanied by a brutal and bloody partition. The former British Indian Empire was divided into two countries: Pakistan, created at the behest of some elements from the Muslim community and in particular its leadership under Muhammad Ali Jinnah, was itself divided into East and West Pakistan, separated by over 1,000 miles of India in between. Partition was accompanied by bloody communal riots which saw roughly 1 million persons killed and massive migrations as some Muslims moved to Pakistan while the overwhelming majority of Hindus and Sikhs located in territory allocated to Pakistan moved to India.

States ruled by royal families were given an option to join India or Pakistan, though some tried to become independent. The princely states of Hyderabad and Jundagh were absorbed into India in 1948 after some armed confrontation. However, the biggest problem came with respect to the princely state of Jammu and Kashmir where a majority Muslim population lived under a Hindu ruler. In this state, the territories of Gilgit and Baltistan fell without a shot being fired when a garrison of Kashmiri troops, under British officers, unilaterally declared allegiance to Pakistan and presented the Maharaja with a fait accompli.

The 1948 Kashmir War[1]

1948 saw a carefully orchestrated military operation in which Pakistani-supported tribesmen staged an invasion of the state, which led to the collapse of the Kashmiri State forces and several instances where Muslim soldiers mutinied and killed their Hindu comrades. Faced with this situation, Maharaja Hari Singh signed an instrument of accession to India. In 1948, the first Kashmir War was fought between the Indian troops and Pakistani Pathans invading from the northwest of the Kashmir region. The conflict ended with an Indian appeal to the UN which led to a ceasefire. India held some two thirds of the state with the rest in Pakistani hands. There was also a mutual agreement to a formation of a Line of Control (LoC), the Ceasefire Line to which the troops of both nations were withdrawn within a short period of time.

The Ceasefire Line, however, had a number of problems, not the least of which was the fact that the maps for the northernmost regions of Kashmir, especially in the Ladakh area, were poorly demarcated: with the division of the territory between India and Pakistan there were additional issues with respect to the uninhabited regions near the Karakoram Range and the Shaksgam Valley. With no presence of people in either these areas or the Aksai Chin region of Ladakh, the situation was further complicated when the People's Republic of China occupied Aksai Chin and began constructing infrastructure in the area.

However, while the LoC was quite viable, the plans for a plebiscite fell apart. It included a number of preconditions which formed part of UN resolution 47 of 1948, dated 21 April 1948.[2] This recommended a non-binding formula aimed at resolving the dispute. Noteworthy in the aforesaid resolution is that the Government of Pakistan should undertake to use its best endeavours:

> To secure the withdrawal from the State of Jammu and Kashmir of tribesmen and Pakistani Nationals not normally resident therein, who have entered the State for the purposes of fighting and to prevent any intrusion into the State of such elements and any furnishing of material aid to those fighting in the State.[3]

The presence of Indian troops was to be reduced to a minimum but they were not to be completely withdrawn.

Ultimately, Pakistan has never withdrawn any troops or citizens from the area concerned. Moreover, the original territorial entity of Jammu and Kashmir no longer exists because:

- Pakistan ceded land to China in the Shaksgam Valley in the state per the 1963 Sino-Pakistan Boundary Agreement; while
- The Askai Chin region has been occupied by China since the 1950s and following the 1962 war between India and China, this territory has remained under Chinese control.

Indeed, the – for India – disastrous war with China in 1962 led to a Line of Actual Control that is not properly demarcated or agreed in parts of Ladakh. In 2020, Chinese transgressions in this area led to clashes and casualties on both sides with a tense armed stand-off being in force to date.

The 1965 War[4]

While India subsequently followed a non-aligned foreign policy, Pakistan became allied to the United States of America (USA), and thus joined the Baghdad Pact, the Central Treaty Organisation (CENTO), and the Southeast Asia Treaty Organization (SEATO), and signed a mutual defence agreement with the USA in 1954. This led to a rise in Pakistan's military and diplomatic influence in Washington as well as to an influx of US arms. Over the following years, India and Pakistan fought two major wars: in August 1965, Pakistan infiltrated close to 30,000 troops into the state of Kashmir. This effort was met with an Indian military counteroffensive and escalated into a general war. This conflict saw the first large-scale use of air power and armour in the subcontinent, and though it ended in a strategic stalemate, the experience gained by both militaries was used to effect in subsequent conflicts. It should be noted that the Kashmir War of 1965 was the last occasion on which Pakistan attempted to use force to wrest the control of Kashmir from India and, coming as it did after India's defeat in the war with China of 1962, probably represented Pakistan's best chance of doing so.[5]

Pakistani forces entered Jammu and Kashmir while Indian forces hit back by crossing the international border. This resulted in a major showdown of armour, airpower and incursions by the Indian Army deep into Pakistan while the Pakistan Army made smaller gains into India. The UN brokered a ceasefire and in 1966, India and Pakistan signed an agreement in Tashkent (in the USSR) to resolve their issues in a peaceful manner. However, the Indian Prime Minister Lal Bahadur Shastri died shortly after and thus the Tashkent Declaration proved ill-fated: it was to have virtually no long-term effect. The only of its points that was realised was the insistence on the observance of the 1948 Ceasefire Line:

> The Prime Minister of India and the President of Pakistan have agreed that all armed personnel of the two countries shall be withdrawn not later than 25 February 1966 to the positions they held prior to 5 August 1965, and both sides shall observe the cease-fire terms on the cease-fire line.[6]

The Ceasefire Line of 1948 was thus formalised into the 'Line of Control': however, as will be discussed in more detail in subsequent chapters the area leading to the Karakoram Range and the Siachen Glacier was not properly demarcated.

1971 India-Pakistan War[7]

Tensions between the two countries continued to flare up, and – following internal crises that degenerated into the systematic repression and mass killings of people in what used to be East Pakistan – the two countries went to war with each other once again. After India supported an armed insurrection in East Pakistan, on 22 November 1971 an armoured clash provoked an air battle. In turn, then-West Pakistan then launched a pre-emptive strike on Indian air bases in the west. In the course of the general war, the Indian armed forces defeated the Pakistan Army and Air Force in East Pakistan, enabling the creation of the independent country of Bangladesh. Simultaneously, Pakistan's attempts to relieve the pressure by attacking India in the west were thwarted and sizeable parts of the country occupied by the Indian Army.

However, and despite numerous suggestions to the contrary, India had no intention of destroying Pakistan in that conflict. Instead, it sought to deliver only enough blows to the Pakistani armed forces to destroy their carefully-cultivated myth of invincibility. The 1971 India-Pakistan War thus marked an important psychological blow to the psyche and prestige of Pakistan and its armed forces.[8] The resulting dismemberment of the country and the armed forces' abject failure to prevent it, led to a deep resolve among many in Pakistan's military and intelligence elites to repay India in kind. That they have not been successful to date, despite making huge efforts to that end, has not caused any rethink in an ultimately self-destructive approach to relations with India.

The 1971 war directly led to the Shimla Declaration of 1972 which aimed at settling all disputes bilaterally. This agreement, signed between Prime Minister Indira Gandhi of India and President Zulfikar Ali Bhutto of Pakistan had three particularly noteworthy elements:

- A mutual commitment to the peaceful resolution of all issues through direct bilateral approaches
- To build the foundations of a cooperative relationship with special focus on people to people contacts
- To uphold the inviolability of the LoC in Jammu and Kashmir, which is a most important confidence-building measure (CBM) between India and Pakistan, and a key to durable peace.[9]

This latter point has been critical to India's approach to the Kashmir dispute. India believes that the Line of Control is to be respected while, as Kargil 1999 showed, Pakistan has a rather different approach and has repudiated the Shimla Accords in most ways, not the least of which is its continued approach to treat the LoC as a boundary to be violated as needed to pursue its own interests. The Shimla Accord represented the last, and undoubtedly, best chance for durable peace between India and Pakistan. Unfortunately, Pakistan's then civilian government was toppled shortly thereafter, with Prime Minister Bhutto being hanged in 1979. The bitterness of defeat, the quest for a cause to justify its power and India's own mistakes internally, allowed the Pakistan military establishment to stir up an insurgency.

India's Security Situation in the 1980s

When Operation Meghdoot was launched in 1984, India was in a state of turmoil that was to last for decades. The country was plagued by issues related to widespread poverty, an economy that was performing modestly, and a drought. However, it was equally at the point where a growing middle class was becoming increasingly assertive and important. This group, well-educated and articulate, began to see a role for India beyond the very limited one that had hitherto been performed by the country and its military in the international arena. This led, not only to a re-evaluation of the country's foreign policy objectives but also an increase in its

Rajiv Gandhi, Prime Minister of India from 1984 to 1989. (National Archives)

Indian Army troops detaining suspects during one of the brutal counterinsurgency operations in Kashmir in the 1980s. (Albert Grandolini Collection)

military forces and a revision of its strategic policy.

Central to India's security is the fact that it is bordered by two countries with which it has serious border disputes: as well as a volatile border with Pakistan, from 1983 to about 1993 a Pakistani-sponsored insurgency erupted in the Indian federal state of Punjab, sparked in the disputed Kashmir region. Moreover, it was the Sino-Pakistan strategic partnership that created significant concerns in New Delhi: by 1986-1987 China showed that it had few qualms about selling missile technology to Pakistan and in an egregious act of nuclear proliferation, it supplied Pakistan with reliable designs for atomic weapons.

Shortly after the end of the Kargil War in 1999, the first photographs appeared of the Indian Army's Bofors FH-77 155mm howitzers deployed in the Siachen area. This is the heaviest piece of armament deployed by any of the involved parties. (Indian Army)

With China, the border dispute was not nearly as serious, though there was and is mutual distrust between Beijing and New Delhi. This has meant that a substantial Indian troop presence has been maintained along the Sino-Indian border ever since the two countries fought a short but vicious war in 1962. There was a sharp clash at Nathu La and Cho La in 1967 in which 88 Indians and over 300 Chinese soldiers were reported killed. In 1975, an incident led to the deaths of four Indian soldiers of the Assam Rifles Regiment in an ambush at Tulung La in Andhra Pradesh. After that, in mid-1987, while the Siachen conflict was ongoing, Chinese and Indian forces were involved in a confrontation at the Sumdrong Chu Valley, prompting then Chief of Army Staff, Krishnaswamy Sundarji, to hold Operation Chequerboard which involved a substantial increase of 50,000 troops to the strength then present in Arunachal Pradesh, and an exercise involving 10 divisions and several squadrons of the Indian Air Force was held. Three divisions at Wangdung were sustained solely by air, thus demonstrating to China a capability to sustain forces in distant areas away from road links and which has proved to be very important for Indian units facing China ever since that date. The confrontation led to no combat between the countries.[10]

Meanwhile, and except in Punjab, substantial insurgencies sprang up and intensified in the form of brutal ethnic violence in Assam, Nagaland, Mizoram, Manipur and even Meghalaya and Tripura, to the Punjab where the Indian Army was compelled in 1984 to storm the holiest of Sikh shrines – the Golden Temple in Amritsar – to neutralise terrorists holed up therein to the increasingly intense protests in Kashmir over rigged elections in 1987.[11] While India's military was heavily committed to internal security operations, however, its forces were still quite able to focus on conventional warfare against its hostile and very capable neighbours.

The Prime Minister of India from 1984 to 1989, was Rajiv Gandhi, the son of the previous Prime Minister, Indira Gandhi, in turn, the daughter of India's first Prime Minister, Jawaharlal Nehru. Indira Gandhi was assassinated in 1984 by her Sikh bodyguards in retaliation for the assault on the Golden Temple. This led to a vicious pogrom against Sikhs in Delhi, aided by the governing Indian National Congress. Rajiv Gandhi won the 1984 elections in a landslide victory and proceeded to begin a haphazard, though well-intentioned, series of economic reforms and an expansion of the armed forces.

Kashmir

Pakistan exploited the rigged 1987 elections for the State Assembly of Jammu & Kashmir to fuel local anti-India resentment. This intensified as Pakistani support to insurgents and terrorists led to India adopting an increasingly harsh line and to launching a relentless counterinsurgency campaign. India also found attempts by some Western powers – the United States of America and Great Britain among them – to try to mediate or equate India with Pakistan particularly galling, and rejected these outright. Although attracting bitter criticism from the West, India's counterinsurgency approach was as unapologetic as Islamabad was unrelenting in its support for insurgent and terrorist groups (which operated from its territory with impunity). Following a spate of Pakistan-instigated terrorist attacks – which culminated in the strike at Pulwama on 14 February 2019 – and an Indian retaliation on 26 February (followed by a lukewarm Pakistani response, a day later), a major shift in the region's status occurred as India's parliament removed the provisions, always deemed temporary since 1953, that gave the Jammu & Kashmir region a special constitutional status. The state was subsequently converted into the two Union Territories of Jammu & Kashmir and Ladakh.

3
THE RIVAL FORCES

The Indian and Pakistani armies have common roots and have a common obsession with their borders in the Punjab and Rajasthan, plus their seemingly intractable dispute over the region that was formerly the princely state of Jammu and Kashmir. However, India has an additional problem with the People's Republic of China, which has made significant incursions into Indian-claimed territory since 1962. India and Pakistan each deploy a brigade sized force – Indian and Pakistani brigades having a strength of between 3,000 and 5,000 personnel – against each other on the Siachen battlefield. It should be noted that India's effort in Siachen has been prodigious, with battalions from every part of the army sending personnel to the Siachen Glacier over the decades. Since 1962, India has been procuring specialised equipment and has raised dedicated mountain formations – albeit tasked for use against China – but these have all been part of the country's effort in the region with formations now being tasked against either adversary. However, both countries have substantially larger forces that can be brought to bear, with India in particular, having a number of dedicated mountain formations that could offer potential reinforcements should a conflict expand. As will be seen in subsequent chapters, the value of Siachen to India's position versus China and Pakistan is crucial and its hold on the glacier also involves the ability to defend very tenuous supply lines. In other words: the risk of an expanded conflict cannot be dismissed and as such the broader formations in both armies will be examined, especially given the recent Indian moves to create a specialised Mountain Strike Corps and in regards of improving and expanding its airlift and combat air support potential in theatre.

Table 1: Indian Army, Order of Battle, 1984-2020

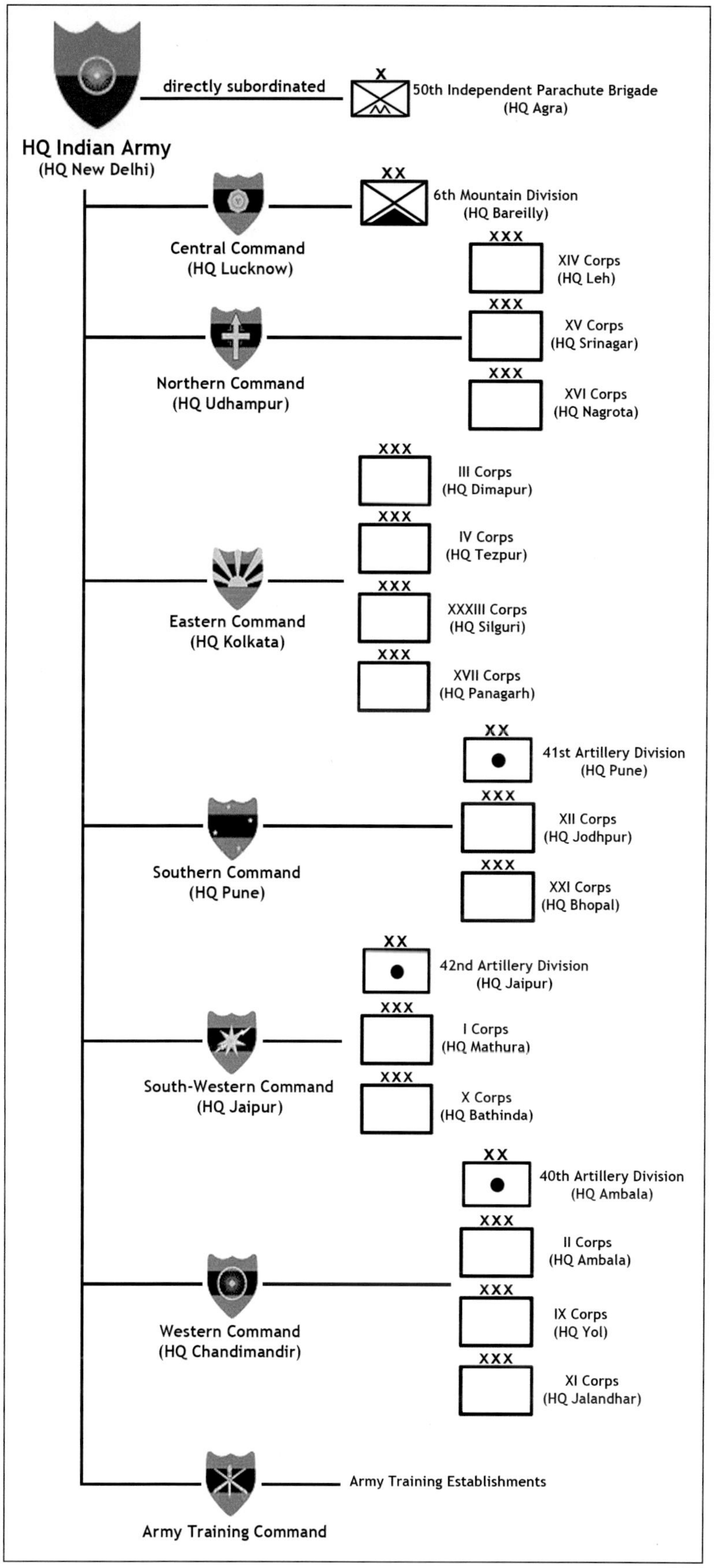

The Indian Army[1]

The Indian Army consists of 11 corps-sized formations, with a total of 36 divisions, and a number of independent brigades. The cutting edge of the Indian Army is centred around three powerful 'strike corps' – each built around one armoured division. The other eight corps are defined as 'holding corps', though they have significant offensive potential.

India has moved, in the period post-2015, to create integrated battlegroups for both mountains and plains. The first of these integrated battlegroups will be assigned to the newly raised Mountain Strike Corps which is specially tasked for deployment against China.

In addition to these combat formations, the Indian Army has four engineer brigades and 14 Army Aviation Corps helicopter units. A separate Corps of Army Air Defence operates six air defence brigades and two surface-to-air missile groups. These elements were assigned to formations on a need basis, though with AAD units in particular, many were earmarked for deployment and operations with specific formations, with priority going to armoured and other mechanized units.

Northern Command; the Command Responsible for Siachen

Following the 1971 India-Pakistan War, the Government of India decided to raise a separate command to oversee operations in the northern borders with Pakistan and China. To this end, a Northern Command was established and Lieutenant General Premindra Singh Bhagat was appointed as the first Army Commander in June 1972. The headquarters for the new command was established at Udhampur, in Jammu and Kashmir.

One of only a few Soviet-made M-46 guns to see deployment and active combat use by the Indian Army during the fighting in the Siachen area. (Indian MOD)

As of the mid-1980s, the Northern Command controlled three corps. The XIV Corps (Leh), XV Corps (Srinagar) and XVI Corps (Nagrota) control the operational units in Northern Command. These corps had responsibility not only for defensive and offensive operations against Pakistan and China, but also for the ongoing counterinsurgency and counterterrorist operations against Pakistani-supported militants. The 1999 Kargil operations fell under the ambit of the Indian Army's Northern Command – in particular XV Corps. In peacetime, the area was the responsibility of 121st (Independent) Infantry Brigade, itself a part of the 3rd Infantry Division, but later attached to the 8th Mountain Division when this assumed a greater share of responsibilities in the Kargil area. This corps had two full infantry divisions attached to it plus an additional artillery brigade at corps level. The 8th Mountain Division had three infantry brigades and one artillery brigade under its command while the two independent brigades – the 121st Infantry and the 50th Parachute – were attached to it temporarily. The other Indian division – the 3rd Infantry – allocated one full brigade and one independent brigade to the operations.

The Siachen Brigade – 102 Infantry Brigade – was established in Partapur and has ever since been headquartered there. It is assigned to 3rd Infantry Division and in that capacity, its 3,000 men have the support of the division with attendant artillery in the form of the 3rd Artillery Brigade, engineering and logistics elements. Even at the height of the Kargil operations, 102 Infantry Brigade was not diverted from its Siachen tasking.

Emphasis on Mountain Warfare

With 11 mountain divisions and three more under rising for the Mountain Strike Corps, the Indian Army has clearly attached much importance to mountain warfare. The growth of the People's Liberation Army of the PRC, its reforms and reorganisations, and the expansion of its presence in the Himalayas since the 1980s have proved to be a major challenge for India.

For India, the main military formation opposing China remains the mountain division, while new technology has been absorbed and there has been significant re-equipment of these units, their basic TOE has remained little changed over the last 30 years. The Indian Army is well-deployed and well-stocked to meet any kind of situation. It has set up an optical fibre network for its own communication in the border areas, has developed a well-considered deployment plan and strong fortifications, and has substantial munition stocks.

The Basic Indian Mountain Division – Organisation and Equipment

India's focus on mountain divisions emerged in the aftermath of the 1962 Sino-Indian War. The lessons of that defeat led India to understand the importance of having specially trained formations that were acclimatised and equipped for mountain warfare. Priority was then accorded to raising and equipping India's mountain divisions.

Like their counterparts in the plains, the mountain divisions have between three and five brigades with attached artillery, signals and engineering formations. However, at battalion level, the then-standard 106mm recoilless guns were replaced by lighter 57mm weapons.

Infantry Weapons

Indian infantry units in 1984 were still armed with the Ishapore 1A1 – a version of the 7.62mm FN FAL – as its primary infantry weapon. Each section of 11 men was also issued with one or two 7.62mm 1B light machine guns (the local version of the L4A4) and one 84mm Carl Gustav recoilless rocket launcher.[2] Platoon-level firepower was augmented by a 51mm mortar and each battalion had eight Ishapore 2A1 7.62mm machine guns (the local version of the FN MAG) assigned to it, along with six 81mm mortars. The Sterling sub-machine gun – known locally as the 9mm 1A1 – remained in widespread service as a personal defence weapon for section leaders. Since 2002 a combination of 5.56mm INSAS rifles and machine guns, plus Kalashnikov variants have replaced the Ishapore SLRs but these are in turn being replaced, rather surprisingly, by a new

7.62mm NATO rifle – the SiG-716 – and the AK-203 for non-infantry personnel.

Battalion support weapons are, in the main, unchanged from the late 1970s with the FN MAG machinegun and 81mm mortars dominating. However, battalion and support company firepower were being augmented with the induction of 30mm AGS-17 automatic grenade launchers of Russian origin, which were to prove invaluable for fire support during the Siachen conflict, with troops deployed there being among the first recipients of the system along with the Dragunov Designated Marksman Rifle. This latter weapon is being supplemented by Beretta .338 Lapua Magnum Scorpio TGT and the Barrett .50 calibre M95 anti-materiel rifle.

The 106mm M40A1 recoilless rifles and 57mm M18 recoilless rifles served until the 1990s but these were completely phased out and replaced at battalion level by MILAN ATGM launchers, augmented by Russian 9K111 Fagot (AT-4 'Spigot') systems. The MILAN, with its MIRA thermal sight, would be used effectively in the direct fire role. Prior to this, SS-11B1 missiles were used on a variety of ground and vehicle mounts to supplement the M40A1. A number of SS-11B1s were sent to the Siachen Glacier for use against bunkers until their replacement with MILANs. For longer-range engagements, the Konkurs-M 9M113M (AT-5B Spandrel) system is used, augmented with supplies of Israeli SPIKE-LR missiles.

Two Indian Army troops at an observation posts in the northern Ladakh in the late 1990s. The one in the foreground is armed with a Sterling sub-machine gun and the one in the rear with one of many versions of the AK-47 Kalashnikov assault rifle. (Albert Grandolini Collection)

An Indian Army soldier with SA-7 MANPAD, seen during deployment in northern Ladakh. (Indian MOD)

Artillery Support

The mountain artillery regiments were – in the past – equipped with either 76mm Yugoslav-made M48 guns, OTO Melara M56 105mm howitzers, or with an Indian-designed 75/24mm howitzer. By the time of the Kargil War, however, all mountain and field regiments were re-equipped with the Indian-designed and manufactured 105mm Indian Field Gun (IFG), or its lighter counterpart, the Indian Light Field Gun (LFG). This has changed significantly with the 130mm M46 field gun now in widespread service alongside the 155/39 Bofors FH77/B02 gun/howitzer which equips 20 artillery regiments, with these guns being the single heaviest artillery piece deployed by India during the Siachen conflict. Augmenting these are 145 US-designed M777 lightweight howitzers which are optimised for use in mountainous terrain.

The Army maintained a force of 40 light regiments, each equipped with a dozen local versions of the Brandt AM-50 mortar and these were assigned initially on the basis of one per division with some additional units earmarked for the mountains. However, this number has now fallen to 25 such regiments as 155mm guns replaced the 105mm IFG in infantry divisions and the latter in turn replaced 120mm mortars. A single heavy mortar regiment was equipped with 160mm Tampella mortars but these were retired in 2021, though this regiment performed with distinction during the 1999 Kargil War.

A group photo of Indian Army troops while on a patrol along the Line of Control. (Indian Army)

be mounted. Each battalion has an integral special forces platoon – the Ghatak platoon – while the elite Special Frontier Force operates as an important force-multiplier.

All of India's Special Forces are also inducting new equipment for operations in high altitude and mountainous areas in the form of new long-range sniper rifles and man-portable anti-tank weapon systems to high-speed underwater scooters and hand-launched micro drones, as India continues to gradually modernise its special forces.

The Parachute Regiment and Parachute Brigade

Most of the Indian Army's Special Forces are grouped into the Parachute Regiment. This has its roots in the Second World War and has many operations to its credit, including a battalion level para drop during the 1971 war and has operated extensively in military operations subsequently.

In 1984, when the Siachen conflict started, the Indian Parachute Regiment was at one and the same time both very similar to its current configuration while being very different. In 1984, the unit had some seven Para battalions – 1, 2, 3, 4, 5, 6 and 7 – as airborne light infantry, a force of jeeps equipped with 106mm M40A1 recoilless rifles, and two field regiments – 9th and 17th – now equipped with Indian-designed 75/24 pack howitzers.

The Parachute Regiment presently has eight Special Forces battalions, five Airborne, two Territorial Army and one counterinsurgency battalion, the Rashtriya Rifles, in its order of battle. The total strength of the regiment stands at about some 4,500 personnel in the Paratroopers (Airborne), while the Para (SF) includes about 1,200 operatives:

The 50th Parachute Brigade comprises the following units:

- 2 airborne infantry battalions
- 1 special forces battalion
- 1 Parachute Field Regiment (Artillery) (9 and 17 Parachute Field Regiments in rotation)
- 60 Parachute Field Hospital
- 411 (Independent) Parachute Field Company (Bombay Sappers)
- 622 Parachute Composite Company (ASC)
- 50th (Independent) Parachute Brigade OFP (Ordnance)
- 50th (Independent) Parachute Brigade Signal Company
- 2 (Independent) Parachute Field Workshop Company (EME)
- 252 (Para) Air Defence Battery
- 50th (Independent) Parachute Brigade Provost Section[6]

The President's Bodyguard also forms part of the brigade as the pathfinders company.

The five airborne infantry battalions of the Parachute Regiment rotate to form part of the brigade, alternatively serving their field tenures in counterinsurgency operations or high altitude areas.

The Mountain Strike Corps[3]

The concept of the Strike Corps was to radically alter the Army's traditionally defensive stance since the humiliating defeat in the 1962 border war with China. It was to be the Indian Army's left and right hook, with the one deployed in Ladakh designed to become a powerful formation backed by artillery, cruise missiles, light tanks, special forces and helicopters, capable of breaking through Chinese defences, crossing over into the Tibetan Plateau, capturing and securing territory that would be a bargaining chip in post-conflict negotiations.

As originally envisaged, the Mountain Strike Corps – or XVII Corps – was to be headquartered in Ranchi with divisions headquartered in Panagarh, West Bengal (59th Mountain, with 16,000 troops) and Pathankot (72nd Mountain), Punjab. Aviation, artillery and armoured brigades were to be integrated into the corps that was planned with entirely new raisings of nearly 30 mountain infantry battalions. In addition, it was also to be reinforced with teams of high altitude Special Forces. Its strength was supplemented with armoured, artillery and air defence, engineer brigades spread from Ladakh to Arunachal Pradesh, with 90,274 personnel.[4] Of these, 59th Mountain Division was fully raised but only one brigade of 72nd Mountain Division was operationalised before financial constraints came to the fore. An additional artillery brigade is now attached to the sub-strength formation. There are ongoing plans to reorientate at least one of the existing Strike Corps to augment forces in Ladakh to enable the fledgling MSC to focus on India's north-eastern frontier with China. India's forces in Siachen therefore have the potential to receive substantial reinforcements from other units with more offensive potential, with the environment being the operating limiting factor.

India's Special Forces[5]

India has made increasing use of its Special Forces to spearhead efforts in difficult terrain and Siachen was and is no exception. The Indian Army, rotating troops through the Siachen Brigade has allowed for the Indian Army's Special Forces to get a level of experience in the region that allows for their use in any offensive operation that might

One of the eight Special Forces battalions serves in the brigade on rotation. One of the two field artillery regiments (9 Para Field Regiment and 17 Para Field Regiment) also forms part of the brigade while the other serves out its field tenure on rotation. These artillery regiments are equipped with 105mm LFG guns while a number of BMP-2 ICVs are also available for paradropping operations as part of the Regiment. The 252 AD Battery uses Igla-1M man-portable SAMs.

The Para Special Forces Battalions[7]

The Para Commando units were created in 1966 by the Indian Army. During the Indo-Pakistani War of 1965, a small ad hoc force comprising volunteers from most infantry units operated along and behind enemy lines. The performance of this force proved to the higher authorities that such forces had much utility and as such there was greater emphasis placed on the raising of unconventional forces.

In 1984, only 9 and 10 Para Commando battalions were in operation. These units received some training in HALO operations, as did a select number of paratroopers.[8] However, while they were the first to be issued with night-vision and night-fighting gear in 1984, this was in acutely short supply. Moreover, while some efforts were being made to equip them with Kalashnikov variants as well as with a limited quantity of Western-origin weapons of 7.62x39mm and 5.56x45mm respectively, the bulk of even these special forces were equipped with standard Indian infantry weapons and their standard rifle was the Ishapore SLR. The Para Commando battalions were developing specialisations with one of the two battalions being tasked for mountain operations and the other for operations in the mountains.

As the Siachen conflict began to intensify, the Para Commando battalions were increasingly in demand for highly skilled personnel to spearhead assaults on enemy positions. As a result, and owing to reorientation, the force was significantly expanded to a force of eight Special Forces battalions.

The Ghatak Platoons

The Ghatak Platoons, or Ghatak Commandos, are a special operations-capable infantry platoon attached on the scale of one such platoon to every infantry battalion in the Indian Army. They have been described as an elite group of infantry, and act as shock troops and spearhead assaults ahead of the rest of the battalion.

A Ghatak Platoon is usually 20 strong and consists of a commanding captain, two non-commissioned officers and some specialists like snipers and spotters, light machine gunners, a medic and a radio operator. The remaining soldiers act as assault troopers for the platoon. As might be expected, only the most physically fit and motivated soldiers in an infantry battalion are selected to be a part of the Ghatak Platoon, and it is mandatory for all of their officers to pass the commando training course.

The Special Frontier Force

While not strictly an Indian Army formation, the Special Frontier Force has played an extremely important role in the Siachen conflict, and in broader operations in Ladakh – both against Pakistan and China. Raised with CIA assistance after the 1962 war with China, the SFF is comprised largely of Tibetan refugees settled or born in India and Gorkhas from Nepal or India, the latter now predominating. The SFF Vikas battalions are well-equipped units, often getting advanced rifles ahead of India's other Special Forces. However, they lack heavy weapons beyond the battalion level and it is a combination of their unique origin, their training and extreme motivation that has made them a formidable force. The SFF thus has a total of six battalions called 1 Vikas, 2 Vikas, 3 Vikas, 5 Vikas, 6 Vikas, and 7 Vikas (there is no 4 Vikas), with each battalion having approximately 800 troops. These six battalions are commanded by Indian Army officers of colonel rank with at least five other Indian Army officers serving in each battalion. The SFF also gets a great deal of assistance from the Indian intelligence agency, the Research and Analysis Wing (RAW), and has access to the said entity's aviation wing – the Aviation Research Centre (ARC). Three Il-76s, two AN-32s, two Bombardier Global Express and two Gulfstream III aircraft – many specially modified with surveillance, ELINT and electronic warfare equipment – are available for use by the ARC.[9]

High Altitude Warfare School – the Siachen Training Facility[10]

All Indian personnel being sent to the Siachen Glacier pass through HAWS. The High Altitude Warfare School (HAWS) was formed in 1948 as a direct result of the loss of the Gilgit-Baltistan region of Kashmir to Pakistan during the Siege of Skardu as part of the broader 1947-1948 Indo-Pakistan War. Initially known as the 19 Infantry Division Ski School, the school was established in December 1948

A section of Indian Army infantry undergoing training on Siachen. (Indian MOD)

A column of Indian Army troops during a training trek along the lower segment of the Siachen Glacier. (Indian MOD)

by General K S Thimayya, who was then a brigadier. In the winter of 1949–50, the school was redesignated as a Command Establishment and renamed as the Winter Warfare School, a title which it held until 8 April 1962, when it was upgraded to a Category A Training Establishment and had its current name attached to it.

The HAWS curriculum offers two programs: the Mountain Warfare Course and the Winter Warfare Course. The former is conducted in Sonamarg between May and October while the latter course is conducted in Gulmarg between January and April. Both courses conduct specialised training in high altitude warfare, counterintelligence and survival skills. In addition, ice-craft is taught at Machoi across Zojila, thus making HAWS invaluable for Siachen operations. Located in the beautiful Gulmarg Valley, HAWS is an extremely demanding institution and some courses have a drop-out rate of 30-40 percent.[11]

The school is also a major participant in avalanche rescue operations. In 2018, several members of the 200-strong team that carried out rescue operation at the Siachen Glacier had their training at HAWS.

The Pakistan Army[12]

India's Siachen rival, Pakistan, is far less invested in developing specialised formations for the mountains. However, the Pakistan Army remains a formidable force with a strong tradition of military operations, a flair for tactical brilliance – as was the case in Kargil 1999 – and possess a strong professional ethos.

The Pakistan Army is organised into nine corps and Force Command Northern Area. These contain 22 divisions, 15 independent brigades (six armoured and nine infantry), nine corps artillery brigades, seven engineering brigades and 15 army aviation squadrons (including two of attack helicopters). In addition, the Pakistan Army has eight air defence brigades. It must be pointed out, however, that Pakistani brigades and divisions are somewhat smaller than their Indian counterparts. The order of battle is listed in Table 2.[13]

Pakistan's two principal fighting formations are Army Reserve North and Army Reserve South. These are an approximate equivalent to the Indian Strike Corps in terms of size and composition. These have, as in the case of their Indian counterparts, a nucleus of a single armoured division and up to two infantry divisions with several independent brigades.[14]

Table 2: Pakistan Army, Order of Battle

Corps	HQ Location	Major Corps Formations
I Corps	Mangla, Punjab	6th Armoured Division (Gujranwala), 17th Infantry Division (Kharian), 37th Infantry Division (Kharian)
II Corps	Multan, Punjab	1st Armoured Division (Pakistan)(Multan), 14th Infantry Division (Okara), 40th Infantry Division (Okara)
IV Corps	Lahore, Punjab	2nd Artillery Division (Pakistan) (Gujranwala), 10th Infantry Division (Lahore), 11th Infantry Division (Lahore)
V Corps	Karachi, Sindh	16th Infantry Division (Pano Aqil), 18th Infantry Division (Hyderabad), 25th Mechanized Division (Malir)
X Corps	Rawalpindi, Punjab	Force Command Northern Areas (Gilgit), 12th Infantry Division (Murree), 19th Infantry Division (Mangla), 23rd Infantry Division (Jhelum), Special Security Division (Chilas)
XI Corps	Peshawar, Khyber Pakhtunkhwa	7th Infantry Division (Peshawar), 9th Infantry Division (Kohat)
XII Corps	Quetta	33rd Infantry Division (Quetta), 41st Infantry Division (Quetta)
XXX Corps	Gujranwala, Punjab	8th Infantry Division (Pakistan)(Sialkot), 15th Infantry Division (Pakistan)(Sialkot)
XXXI Corps	Bahawalpur, Punjab	26th Mechanized Division (Bahawalpur), 35th Infantry Division (Bahawalpur)
Army Air Defence Command	Rawalpindi, Punjab	3rd Air Defence Division (Sargodha), 4th Air Defence Division (Malir)
Army Strategic Forces Command	Rawalpindi, Punjab	21st Artillery Division (Pano Aqil), 22nd Artillery Division (Sargodha)

Pakistan's X Corps – Deployed to Siachen

The X Corps is the primary Pakistan Army formation involved in the Siachen conflict, through which brigades are rotated as necessary. The corps was raised in 1974 by Lieutenant-General Aftab Ahmad Khan and is headquartered in Rawalpindi. Ever since, X Corps has had responsibility for operations in some areas of Kashmir, replacing the old system where formations in Kashmir were controlled directly from the General Headquarters (GHQ): this reflects the increasing troop-levels in the area plus the increased importance given to operations therein. The X Corps is in control of three divisions:

- 23rd Infantry Division (HQ Jehlum)
- 12th Infantry Division (HQ Murree)
- Force Command Northern Areas, Gilgit-Baltistan (HQ Gilgit)

As can be seen, Pakistan, not facing a threat from China, has not had to invest in dedicated mountain formations to the extent that India has done. However, the three formations attached to X Corps are well equipped and prepared for their tasks and are equipped to a standard similar to that of their Indian counterparts. While Pakistan's artillery and infantry units facing India along most of their shared frontiers have received advanced 155mm and 203mm artillery pieces, Pakistan's mountain units have been known to deploy older 3.7-inch pack howitzers alongside more modern weapons on the Siachen Glacier and while the Pakistan Army is a modern and well-equipped force, it has not emphasised mountain artillery to the same extent as India.[15]

As to the ability of Pakistan's mountain infantry, it should be noted that the burden of the Kargil campaign was borne by the Northern Light Infantry which is headquartered at Gilgit in Gilgit-Baltistan. Four NLI battalions – 5, 6, 8 and 12 – were deployed in full strength while elements of 3, 4, 7 and 11 NLI together with the Chitral and Bajaur Scouts were employed for logistic support of the four combatant NLI infantry battalions deployed. These were under the control of 62 Brigade Pakistan Army and were provided with fire support from some 20 Pakistan Army artillery batteries.

Each NLI sub-unit involved in the infiltration was provided with lavish quantities of battalion level support weaponry.[16] The NLI performed very well in the Kargil operations, despite their eventual defeat and they have demonstrated an ability for mountain warfare that is very creditable.

Pakistan's infantry was equipped with locally manufactured G-3 and Type 56 assault rifles, with the MG3 being its standard machinegun. Large numbers of magazine-fed Chinese Type 56 light machineguns were also in widespread service and battalion support weapons were comparable to their Indian counterparts. Pakistani infantry also made extensive use of heavy machineguns for use in the surface role. These were a combination of .50"cal/12.7mm Browning M2HB machineguns and Chinese made copies of the 12.7mm DShK of Soviet origin. Pakistani forces also made extensive use of jeep-mounted 106mm recoilless rifles and US-made BGM-71 TOW ATGMs.

Special Forces

Pakistan's Army Special Service Group, a highly capable unit of some eight battalions, has not developed a specific expertise in high altitude warfare, but is regularly deployed in Siachen. Their deployment, seen from the earliest days of India's Operation Meghdoot, were evident when the SSG launched the unsuccessful Operation Ababeel to pre-empt India. A twelve-man team, led by Captain Muhammad Iqbal hiked at an altitude of 19,000 feet to reach the Indian base camp but were beaten back.[17] The SSG are formidable force with considerable combat experience and have traditionally performed well in combat operations.

Table 3: Pakistan Army, SSG, Order of Battle, 2020[18]

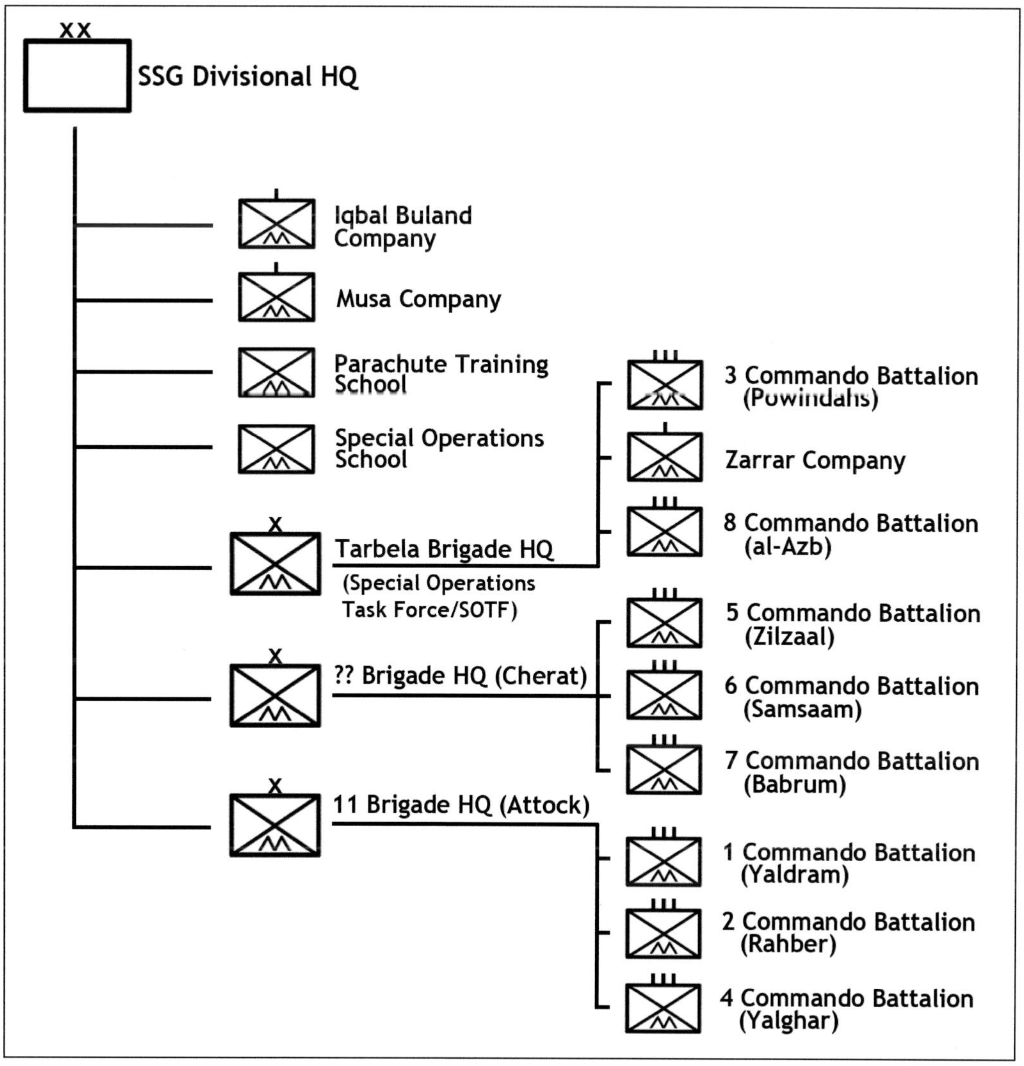

The only official source on the structure of the SSG is a YouTube video which suggests that the force structure is as shown in Table 3, reflecting the tasks of the formation.

Air Support: Challenges facing both Sides

India's Evolving Air Support to Siachen – 1980s to early 2021: Continuity and Change

India's operations in the Siachen Glacier are supported by a prodigious air transport effort. This started in the 1980s and has been enhanced as the decades evolved. The number of assets involved remains the same but the sophistication of the effort has increased. The air support effort is required to support a mere brigade sized formation, but the high altitude deployment means that the logistical strain and effort for this is very taxing for the personnel and aircraft involved, with accidents being an ever-present danger.

In the 1980s, the IAF's transport assets were substantial but largely tactical in nature. Other helicopter assets for the transport role included one unit with Mi-26 heavy lift helicopters (126 HU) and eight with a combination of Mi-8/-17 helicopters which could also be armed with 57mm rocket pods.

The Mi-8/-17 units were to prove their worth during Operation Pawan in Sri Lanka but for Siachen the helicopters lacked the altitude performance of the smaller Cheetahs. However, they remained a useful asset for proximate interventions. The Mi-8/-17 replaced the Mi-4 helicopter in IAF service and has proven to be the most effective medium-lift helicopter operated by the IAF since its inception.[19]

The HAL-built HS.748 filled a multiplicity of tasks with some 60 aircraft being in IAF service, also aided in the carriage of freight, the transport of personnel and liaison tasks. Though not designed as a military transport, the type performed good service for the IAF and remains in service to date, despite its evident shortcomings.[20]

From 1984, the Indian Air Force began receiving An-32 tactical transports and their induction into some six squadrons was able to completely transform the IAF's airlift capabilities with their enhanced payload and troop transport capabilities. The AN-32 was reportedly specially aimed at the Indian market as the AN-26 was deemed by the IAF to have a wholly inadequate performance from 'hot and high' airfields.[21]

Strategic airlift in 1984 was provided by one squadron of AN-12 (No. 25) and one of Il-76 (No. 44) heavy transports. Sufficient Il-76 aircraft would be obtained to allow the conversion of one flight of No. 25 Squadron (the other operating AN-32s) but in the 1980s, the AN-12 and Il-76 reigned as the IAF's long-range transport assets and were to prove decisive during supply operations to India's Northern Command.[22]

The Present – Improved Capability but Similar Challenges[23]

The Indian Air Force in 2020 operates a large transport fleet that numbers well over 200 aircraft. The bulk of the transport fleet consists of seven squadrons operating over 100 AN-32 medium transport aircraft of which a substantial number have undergone a deep upgrade which will be extended to the whole fleet. Forty aircraft were upgraded in Kiev, Ukraine and an additional 15 have been upgraded by 1 BRD of the IAF.

The heavy transport fleet, which includes six Il-78 aerial refuelling aircraft, comprises modest quantities of Il-76s (17), C-130s (12) and C-17s (10 +1). The C-130 is the smallest of the three but has significantly more capacity than the AN-32 and as such cannot be considered medium transports. The C-17 was purchased to augment the Il-76 fleet which has been in service for several decades but with C-17 production being halted, the fleet is unlikely to grow any further and replacements of the Il-76 will be many years in the future.[24]

The IAF helicopter fleet is large and diverse. The backbone of the fleet is provided by no fewer than 151 Mi-17V5 helicopters with possibly 48 more to be ordered. These augment some 160 Mi-17s and between the two variants of the basic Mi-17, completely dominate the Indian medium helicopter inventory with no signs of either dissatisfaction or replacement plans on the part of the IAF. The Mi-17s have also been armed with machine guns and unguided rockets to give them a useful combat capability as demonstrated in 1999.[25]

Heavy transport capability rests with one unit of four Mi-26 helicopters though their replacement with 15 Chinook helicopters is already in progress with deliveries of the Chinook having been completed.

Light observation and liaison tasks are performed by six units of Chetak and two of Cheetah helicopters and though still delivering excellent service, the two types are in dire need of replacement. It is anticipated that HAL's Light Utility Helicopter and the Kamov Ka-226 will share both the IAF and Indian Army's requirement for the type.

Several helicopter units also operate the HAL Dhruv in the light transport role. The Dhruv was always envisaged to have a major role for high altitude operations and with its advanced avionics, and its increased payload capacity as against the Cheetahs. In the role of a light transport, surveillance and casualty

Helicopter support is absolutely essential for survival of the troops in the Siachen area. This Cheetah of the 114 HU, Indian Air Force, was captured on video while bringing supplies to a forward observation post. (Indian Army)

evacuation helicopter, the Dhruv, especially in its Mk.3 version, has proved very effective.

Attack helicopters have never figured prominently in the IAF's fleet and only two helicopter units were equipped with Mi-25 and Mi-35 helicopters respectively. Some of the former have been transferred to the Afghan air force. Replacement of the two types by 22 Apache helicopters, 12 being of the Longbow variant is in progress with the first eight Apaches already inducted. A requirement for an additional 65 attack helicopters is likely to be met by HAL's Light Combat Helicopter.[26]

Sixteen armed Rudra helicopters – a variant of the Dhruv – are also being delivered with eight having been delivered to the IAF in 2017. The armed helicopter fleet of the IAF is thus likely to see a significant improvement in capability as well as an expansion in its fleet of combat assets very soon.[27]

Army Aviation Corps

For decades, the Army Aviation Corps was a large but poorly equipped outfit and when the Siachen conflict started, it was non-existent, being raised only in 1986 and taking over most of the Air Force's Chetak and Cheetah assets. By early 2021 the force operated some 300 helicopters, most of which are Chetak and Cheetah helicopters for light transport and liaison duties as well as reconnaissance and observation. Twelve of a modified Cheetah, called the Lancer, fulfil the light attack role with heavy machine guns and rockets in two pods. However, alongside these light helicopters are an increasing number of HAL Dhruvs of various incarnations with at least 80 such helicopters on strength in five squadrons alongside some 50 armed-Rudra variants. The most recent order for six Boeing AH-64 Apache heavy attack helicopters will dramatically enhance the AACs assets as will the delivery of 10 light combat helicopters from HAL.[28]

At altitudes of 18,000 feet, the payload capacity of the Cheetah helicopter allows for the carriage of only two soldiers and rations. To enable a build up and proper sustaining of the force, the Indian Air Force uses a relay system whereby medium-lift Mi-17 (earlier Mi-8) helicopters ferry supplies to lower altitudes and thereafter Cheetahs move supplies to high altitude positions.

The load carried by Cheetahs could be as low as 25kg and as such many sorties would be needed to accomplish even modest logistical and transport feats. The arrival of the Dhruv, with its improved performance, more powerful engine and better avionics dramatically improves the ability of the IAF and Army Aviation Corps to conduct operations at these extreme altitudes and in poor weather, though the risk of accidents is still very high.[29]

Potential Combat Support – the 1980s and 1990s

No combat assets have ever been deployed by the IAF in the Siachen region – whether in 1984 or since. However, the potential was always there in the event hostilities escalated. In the 1980s, well past the commencement of the Siachen conflict, the IAF had no combat assets in the Siachen theatre. However, the potential of using air support through the Indian Air Force of the mid-1980s was perhaps close to the peak of the number of operational units: it has since significantly improved the quality of the equipment operated through the introduction of Mirage 2000s and Jaguars, followed by MiG-29s.[30]

Three squadrons of Jaguar fighter-bombers were operational by the mid-1980s but the high altitude performance of the type was

A MiG-23MF of the IAF firing a single R-23R semi-active radar homing air-to-air missile. This MiG variant was acquired in reaction to the US sale of General Dynamics F-16s to Pakistan in the mid-1980s, and operated by Nos. 223 and 224 Squadrons, but proved a disappointment in service. Eventually, it was completely withdrawn from service and replaced by MiG-29s. (via Tom Cooper)

The Franco-British SEPECAT Jaguar fighter-bomber was the primary interdiction-strike platform of the IAF as of the mid-1980s. The IAF acquired a total of 40 Jaguars manufactured in Great Britain and 120 produced under licence by HAL. In IAF service the type was nicknamed the Shamsher. (BAE Heritage, via Tom Cooper)

poor. [31] These were augmented with six squadrons of MiG-23s, four of these were tactical strike squadrons with MiG-23BNs and two more were interceptor squadrons with MiG-23MFs. The MiG-27 being manufactured by Hindustan Aeronautics Limited, would eventually equip no fewer than six Indian Air Force squadrons. Among the items of ordnance obtained for the MiG-27 fleet were Kh-25, Kh-25MP, Kh-29L and Kh-23 missiles.[32]

The MiG-21, which peaked at some 19 squadrons in the 1980s, provided a potential force of strike and air defence assets. Alongside these supersonic combat assets were four squadrons of vintage platforms. A single squadron – No. 20 – continued to fly the Hawker Hunter (which also served as an advanced trainer) – while three more – Nos. 2, 22 and 28 – continued to fly the HAL Ajeet in the close support role. These aircraft were of limited capability but were all capable of carrying unguided rockets and bombs in the close support role. However, there was some work done in integrating the R-60 missile with the Hawker Hunter.[33] The Hunters and the Ajeets were to continue in front line service, until 1991 in the case of the Ajeets, and 1998 in the case of the Hunters.

The older aircraft such as MiG-21s, MiG-23s and MiG-27s were found to perform poorly at such altitudes – even more so with the Jaguar. However, the Hawker Hunter was deployed to Leh in 1984 and No. 221 squadron with MiG-23BNs was alerted in case support was needed during Operation Meghdoot. Furthermore, in 1985–86, No. 224 squadron with MiG-23MFs was deployed to Leh to provide air defence cover to the Siachen Glacier while MiG-29s and Mirage 2000s were all deployed to Leh on occasion.

The 1999 Kargil Conflict demonstrated the limitations of the IAF's high altitude strike capability with rocket attacks from MiG-27s, MiG-23BNs and MiG-21s being not particularly effective until new methods of weapon delivery were tested. The Mirage 2000s came into their own as a strike asset with laser guided bombs and computer assisted delivery of 500kg and 250kg bombs. In the aftermath of the Kargil Conflict, India began to pay closer attention to the ability of its combat assets to operate effectively at extreme altitudes.

The pilot of an Aérospatiale SE.315 Lama helicopter of the Pakistan Army Aviation Corps seen after landing at a forward position close to the Siachen Glacier. (Pakistan Army)

Pakistan's Air Support

As of 1984, the Pakistan Air Force had next to no capability to support the army operations in the Siachen area: the available combat aircraft – such as the Shenyang F-6C, Dassault Mirage IIIEP and Mirage 5P – were deemed unsuitable for any effective combat role even over most of Kashmir, and the PAF was forced to cautiously husband its resources in the event that the conflict would escalate. An exception were

Another important helicopter type in service with the Pakistan Army is the Aérospatiale SE.316B/C Alouette III: this example was also photographed during a stop high up in the Himalayas. (Pakistan Army)

IAF's and PAF's new Assets in early 2021[34]

By early 2021, the Indian Air Force has an effective strength of 31 combat squadrons with three additional units being raised and made operational. These include 13 squadrons equipped with Su-30MKI, three each of the MiG-29 and Mirage 2000 (currently undergoing an upgrade), six with Jaguar (at the initial stage of an upgrade process), one of the Tejas LCA (with another forming), one Rafale squadron being formed (with another on order), four with upgraded MiG-21Bison and one solitary squadron of the MiG-21bis.[35] The Rafale promises to give the IAF a truly effective multi-role platform for the 21st century and has come equipped with the full range of air-to-air and air-to-surface munitions.

In a marked difference to the large but somewhat limited force of the 1980s, the IAF is moving towards a much more sophisticated combat force with all the aircraft being increasingly capable of multi-role operations. More important is the fact that the IAF has now moved to employ its aircraft out of its airbases in Ladakh – Leh being the highest such operational base. This has now completely changed and the IAF is now capable of providing a high level of combat air support and with the activation of new air bases and advanced landing grounds, along with the enhanced performance of combat aircraft, the IAF can now provide significant combat support to Indian forces in Siachen and Ladakh.[36]

In similar fashion, it is only since the early 21st century that the PAF is capable of providing effective fire support to the ground forces at hight altitude. Units deploying its most-potent type – the Lockheed-Martin F-16 Fighting Falcon – are known to fly regular combat air patrols (CAPs). However, during the Kargil War of 1999, their operations were severely curtailed by US sanctions following Pakistan's nuclear tests: spares were thus in short supply.[37] As a result, the PAF F-16 force was reduced to flying random CAPs which themselves ended up being discontinued after only a week, during which time PAF F-16s were locked-on to by IAF radars from both Mirage 2000s and MiG-29s. On one occasion Flight-Lieutenant Gaurav Chibber, flying a MiG-29 that was providing top cover for a strike package consisting of MiG-27s, locked-on to two PAF F-16s causing them to abort their intercept attempt.[38]

With newer assets like the F-16C/D and even the CAC/PAC JF-17 in its various versions, the PAF is quite capable of offering highly effective support to the Pakistan Army in the event that such efforts become necessary.[39]

Both air forces are well-trained, highly-motivated and innovative formations that can adapt themselves to any task that might arise. However, as might be expected, any escalation on the glacier involving offensive air power would probably mean an escalation elsewhere along the India-Pakistan frontier, both the Indian and Pakistani air forces would be committed elsewhere, leaving only limited assets for operations near the glacier.

In response to the IAF's Multi-Role Combat Aircraft requirement, and following extensive deliberations and negotiations, New Delhi eventually placed an order for 36 Dassault Rafale fighter-bombers in 2016. Deliveries began in July 2020, and so far all the examples handed over have been Rafale DHs: a two-seat variant similar to the Rafale F3, but with an advanced strike capability. Unsurprisingly, they are arriving together with a wide range of the most advanced air to-air and air-to-ground weaponry and sensors. (Indian Air Force)

Developed in cooperation between the Chengu Aircraft Corporation (CAC) and the Pakistan Aeronautical Complex (PAC), the JF-17 Thunder fighter-bomber serves as a replacement for older Shenyang A-5 and F-7s, Mirage III/5s, and as a complement to the superior F-16s. While up to 60 percent of the airframe is made in Pakistan, all the technologically-demanding parts (primarily including avionics) are made in China, while engines are Klimov RD-33s imported from Russia. (Pakistan Air Force)

The third type that the Pakistan Army deploys for supporting its troops high up in the mountains is the Aérospatiale SA.330B/C/J Puma, up to 45 of which have been acquired since the mid-1970s. (Pakistan Army)

helicopters. The latter included a total of some 18 Alouette IIs and 45 Aérospatiale SA.330B/C Pumas and were used in much the same way the IAF was utilising its Chetaks and Cheetahs. It is only during the last 30 years that 48 Mil Mi-17s were acquired to bolster the Army Aviation Corps. That said, with Pakistan's position on the glacier being at a somewhat lower altitude, and the helicopter fleet of its Army being smaller and thus more concentrated, this allowed for strenuous efforts involving flying and ground personnel.

While Pakistan has tested deployments of combat aircraft to forward operating bases closer to the Siachen Glacier ever since, the PAF has never carried out any related exercises, and thus demonstrated no capability to support ground forces by its air power.

4
OPERATIONS MEGHDOOT AND ABABEEL

The path to the Siachen conflict was one which seemingly emerged out of nowhere. Yet, in a strange sense it was an inevitable consequence of the 1971 India-Pakistan War and the subsequent failure to understand the importance of fully demarcating the Line of Control. It might be forgiven considering the inhospitable terrain and the perceived lack of importance to the decision makers at the time. However, in the mid-1970s, a series of apparently innocuous events were to conspire to push the two countries towards armed conflict. It all started with few maps and an innocent German rafting expedition.

Cartography to Combat

In the aftermath of the 1971 war, and perhaps still smarting from its defeat, Pakistan made some initial attempts to establish 'cartographic control' of the Siachen Glacier, attempting to join the last point on the Line of Control (Point NJ 9842) to the Karakoram Pass, a cartographic line moving north-eastwards. This, to India's thinking was at odds with the terms of the accession of Jammu and Kashmir to India in October 1947 and the Karachi Agreement of 1949 which described the Ceasefire Line (now the Line of Control) beyond Point NJ 9842 (which is the Saltoro Ridge and beyond) to be running northwards (as against north-eastwards) to the glaciers.[1]

Pakistan, whether inadvertently or by design, threw down the gauntlet that led to the Siachen conflict when, in 1975, a German expedition wanted to go rafting on the Indus River in Ladakh. To facilitate the expedition, an Indian Army mountaineer, the legendary Colonel Narinder Kumar (nicknamed 'Bull'), obtained maps of the region from a number of sources and realised that Pakistan had cartographically claimed the Siachen Glacier and made cartographic alterations to the map of the Karakoram Range. This set in train a sequence of events that led to India staging one of its most audacious and bold military operations in 1984.

Colonel Kumar's accounts of events in 1975 indicate that the two Germans who wanted to go rafting were keen to be the first to perform such a feat on the Indus and the then Chief Minister of the erstwhile state of Jammu and Kashmir – Sheikh Abdullah – recommended that they contact Colonel Kumar to assist them. As Sheikh Abdullah was keen to facilitate the success of the first rafting expedition along the Indus, he cleared all the necessary permits in an expedited manner – the norm being clearances for any foreigners being required from the Army as well as the Home Department of Jammu and Kashmir, with the latter issuing the needed 'inner-line permit'.[2] For the Germans, Sheikh Abdullah ordered that the permits be given without Army clearance. The rafting expedition went ahead

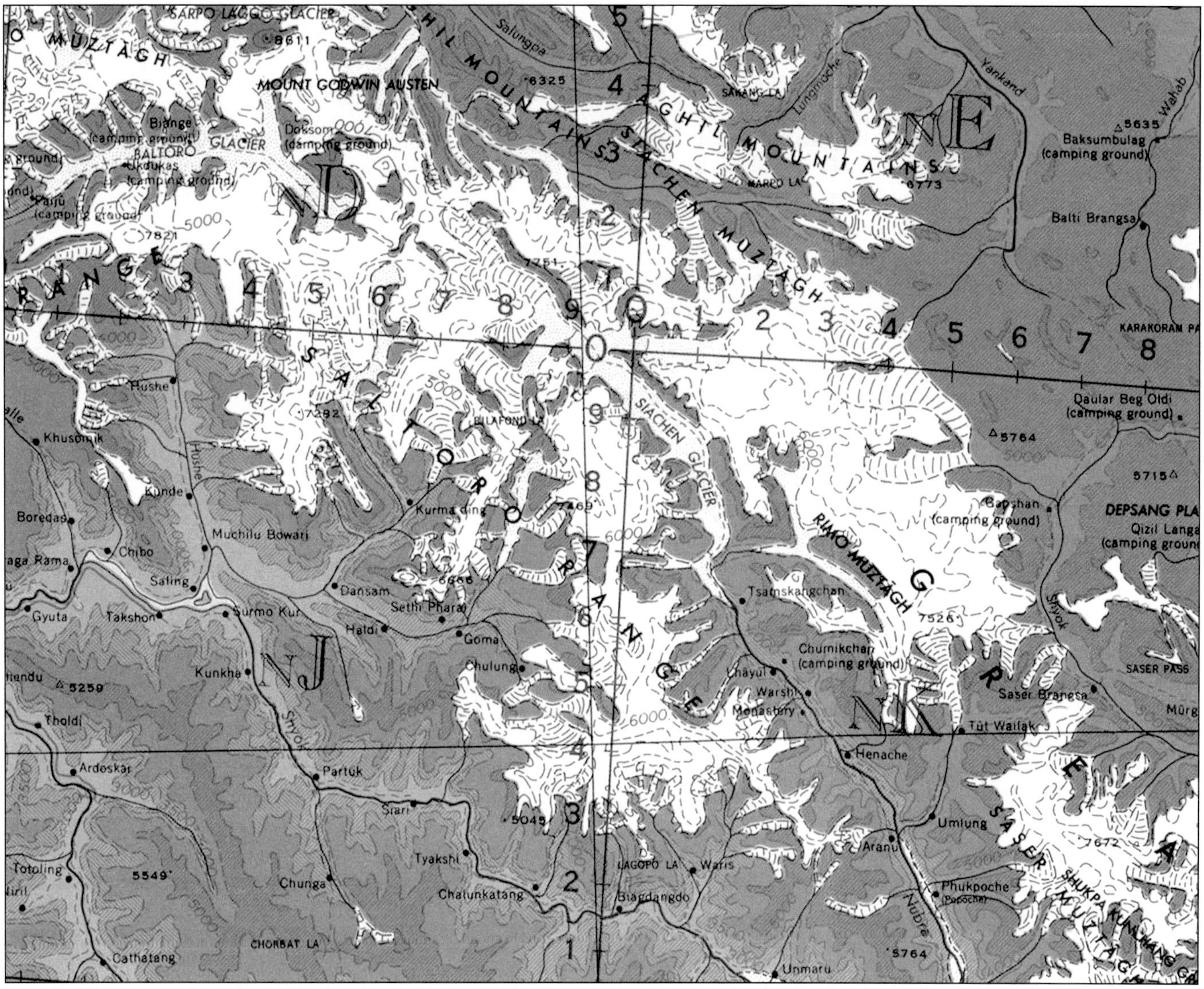

Part of a US Army map from the 1950s, showing the Siacen Glacier. Notably, the map contained no borders, lines of control or otherwise. (US Army)

without problems and the Germans, with Indian assistance, were able to raft from Chumathang to Khalsi – the latter being the point where the Indus goes into Pakistan – in five days. Needless to say, there were a number of excitable newspaper headlines ranging from the tame to the idiotic 'Spying down the River Indus'.[3]

In 1977, after a stint as Commandant of the Indian Army's High Altitude Warfare School (HAWS), Kumar was approached by the same German tourists again, this time with a desire to go rafting down the Nubra River that drains out from the Siachen Glacier. This was not something that had hitherto been attempted, but he began to plan the expedition. The Germans had brought some American maps with them and Kumar – attached to military intelligence since 1961, following a severe bout of frostbite from a mountaineering expedition, and very familiar with cartographic representations of the area – promptly noticed that these showed the LoC extending from the north-east of NJ9842, all the way to the Karakoram Pass. This was in opposition to the agreement for the LoC to follow the natural ridgeline northwards. Before anybody else in India knew it, Kumar realised that Pakistan was now claiming the Siachen Glacier.[4]

After persuading the Germans to leave their maps behind – and paying a substantial sum for them – Kumar went to the Indian Army's Director Military Operations (DMO), Lieutenant-General M.L. Chibber who, thinking to dismiss him, sent him to Brigadier Mehta, one of the Deputy Director Generals in the Operations Directorate. Using his apparently strong powers of persuasion, Colonel Kumar persuaded Brigadier Mehta to refer to treaties from the era of the great Sikh Maharaja, Ranjit Singh and the East India Company, to the Shimla Agreement between Indira Gandhi and Zulfikar Ali Bhutto and – with reference to these treaties and the new maps – Mehta was convinced that Kumar was correct.[5]

The two of them then approached Lieutenant-General Chibber with the ominous news that there were issues with the new American maps and that there were major security implications for India. With reality dawning upon him, Chibber was immediately concerned that India had no information as to what Pakistan had been doing in the region since 1963 – when they ceded territory to China – and to this end, he approached the then Chief of Army Staff, General T.N. Raina, to sanction an expedition for 1978, led by Kumar and run under the guise of it being an operational patrol to enable the Army to provide logistical support to the colonel and his team.[6]

As might be expected, mountaineering expeditions at that altitude and in that terrain, would be prohibitively expensive. Raising money for such an expedition from private funds or getting an official sanction from the Indian government for a civilian expedition would have meant an extended delay. Given Colonel Kumar's concerns about Pakistan's cartographic annexation of Indian territory and the concerns that the Indian Army had about the American maps, the subterfuge in masking the expedition as an operational patrol was completely understandable and, more to the point, completely successful.

Colonel Kumar's plans included the expedition traversing the whole Nubra Valley, the Siachen Glacier and scaling the crest of Karakoram to reach Teram Kangri, noting, the complete absence of Indian troops in the area. Beginning their expedition at the end of August 1978, Colonel Kumar's team of Indian Army mountaineers reached the Teram Kangri-II peak on 13 October 1978.[7] This marked the first time that India had established any presence in this region and, despite Pakistan having ceded the Shaksgam Valley to China in 1963, India had now demonstrated, at least nominally, its continuing claim to it. More importantly, however, the Indian public now became aware that the Siachen Glacier existed and that it belonged to India. This set the stage for tensions with Pakistan leading up to Operation Meghdoot in 1984.

It is also of interest to note that in September 1981, India achieved another feat – the first helicopter landing on the Siachen Glacier. Manmohan Bahadur (who retired as an Air Vice Marshal) was then a Flying Officer with 114 HU flying Chetak helicopters out of Jammu. While originally formed with 10 Chetak helicopters, 114 HU would eventually transfer to Cheetah helicopters but in 1978, Flying Officer Bahadur was tasked with flying over the Siachen Glacier. On 20 September 1978, the Chetak flown by Bahadur and the detachment commander Squadron Leader KDS Sambyal was assigned to drop supplies to the expedition led by Colonel Kumar. This first sortie was followed by several others, culminating in the first helicopter landing on the glacier on 6 October 1978 by Chetak Z-1410 flown by Squadron Leader Monga and FO Bahadur.[8]

In April 1981, Colonel Kumar and a team went back to the Siachen Glacier with the blessings and support of the Chief of Army Staff who ensured that equipment and funding was available, including foreign equipment purchased from Nepal. This expedition took a number of months and the team, despite extreme climatic problems, was able to complete its task and returned in August 1981.

One of the most important outcomes of Colonel Kumar's 1978 and 1981 expeditions was to give Northern Command, and by extension the Indian Army and government an idea about the number of civilian expeditions coming into Siachen via Skardu and Gilgit which fell under Pakistani control. Pakistan was, as part of its attempt to exert cartographic claim over the Siachen Glacier, attempting to encourage mountaineering expeditions in the Karakoram Range, this being ostensibly for the promotion of tourism in their northern areas. This effort led to Pakistani maps extending the Line of Control from NJ 9842 to the Karakoram Pass, thus placing the Siachen Glacier as part of Pakistan.[9]

Pakistan accompanied this effort with a sustained campaign to promote the region to mountaineering tourists, enticing them with the prospect of some of the world's highest peaks. Encouraged by this effort, at least five Japanese and one American expedition were allowed to cross the Saltoro Ridge going through Sia La and Bilafond La, thus enabling them to explore the Siachen Glacier.[10] During the period 1975 to 1978, India took little notice of these Pakistani efforts but, this changed when, after his 1978 expedition, Colonel Kumar established India's physical claim. This somewhat non-confrontational approach, using mountaineering expeditions to establish claims and control was adopted up to 1983. It was in this year that India built its first structure on the glacier and this provided the beginning of the end of the period of peaceful cartographic disputes and expeditions.[11]

In August 1982, however, India began to make preliminary plans for a possible deployment of military forces. This initially took the form of intensified training at the High Altitude Warfare School but then this began, perhaps drawing inspiration from Colonel Kumar and his daring expeditions, with a series of operations to another high altitude mountain range on the other end of India – the Gorichen Peak of Arunachal Pradesh, the highest peak in eastern India, situated between the Tawang and West Kameng districts of that state. This peak is some 6,488 metres (22,500 feet) in height.[12] Arunachal Pradesh is ostensibly claimed by China but India has fully incorporated the region, stationing a garrison there. The Gorichen Range was described by Brigadier D.K. Khanna in the following terms:

> The Gorichen Range is a massive rocky range of mountains with perennial snow. The Gorichen Peak, Point 6488 on the map, has three features emanating from it. They are Point 6338 in the west, Point 6226 to the north and Point 6222 in the south east. The base of the feature is engulfed with precarious crevasse strewn glaciers.[13]

The 19th Battalion of the Kumaon Regiment was assigned to 5 Mountain Division in 1982. This unit was responsible for the defence of the Kameng Frontier Division of Arunachal Pradesh since the war between India and China in 1962. The formation was experienced, familiar with its terrain and area of responsibility but, Major General Sami Khan, the GOC of 5 Mountain Division, was keen that the Gorichen Peak, being the highest peak of the highest range of mountains in his area of responsibility be conquered by troops from his division and to this end, he ordered an expedition to Gorichen.[14]

Though there were problems when the designated team leader fell ill, Khanna, as CO of 19 Kumaon, volunteered to put together a team to scale the Gorichen Peak. Major General Khan was somewhat reluctant to sanction an expedition without an experienced leader, but he gave his approval subject to a detailed administrative plan being prepared by Khanna and submitted to the Adjutant and Quartermaster General of the Division. Khanna was keen on the expedition to familiarise himself with terrain under his battalion's area of responsibility and to build spirit and camaraderie in his new battalion.[15]

With his plan duly approved, personnel were selected and moved to Bombilla where only the best and most fit were selected for the actual expedition. Forty personnel were prepared for the Gorichen Expedition Team – all were 19 Kumaon except for Sepoy Ram Singh of 8 Garhwal Rifles. The expedition left Bombilla on 12 September 1982 and moved to the base camp at Changla – at an altitude of 3,800 metres (12,467 feet). Five days later, it moved to Camp 2 at Phulgan which was at an altitude of 4,400 metres (14,436 feet) where third stage acclimatisation was done.[16]

The Gorichen Expedition Team was able to gradually move to higher elevations and on 26 September established its final base camp at an elevation of 5,000 metres (16,404 feet) to prepare for the final onslaught on Gorichen. Not taking any chances, the team spent much effort in honing ice-craft skills and further improving acclimatisation. This enabled the team to scale Gorichen Peak on 6 October 1982 from two assault camps nearer the summit. This effort marked an important, albeit at the time unknown, step towards preparing for the capability to scale the Siachen Glacier and station troops there.[17]

Polar Bear to Protest Notes

In the summer of 1983, India decided that it needed to keep a closer watch on the Siachen Glacier. Two patrols – Polar Bear 1 and Polar Bear 2 – were thus sent between June and September 1983. Polar Bear 2 was authorised to build a small shelter and a hut was constructed to protect the patrol from strong winds prevalent on the glacier. Though the patrols were noticed by Pakistani helicopters, which duly 'buzzed' them, there was no physical action taken by Pakistan to assert any level of control or to stop the Indian patrols on the Siachen Glacier. The Polar Bear 2 patrol returned to its base by the end of September 1983.[18]

Though Northern Command was pleased with the efforts of the two patrols, it quickly became apparent that Pakistan was not happy. Their Northern Sector Commander sent two strongly worded notes that were an ominous portent of things to come. The first note, sent on 21 August 1983, for the first time claimed all areas northwest of the line joining NJ 9842 to the Karakoram Pass as Pakistan's:

> Request instruct your troops to withdraw beyond Line of Control south of line joining Point NJ 9842, Karakoram Pass NE 7410 immediately. I have instructed my troops to show maximum restraint. But any delay in vacating our territory will create a serious situation.[19]

In response, Northern Command rejected this unilateral extension of the Line of Control and rigorously protested the aerial incursions by Pakistani military helicopters.

Pakistan, as might be expected, did not acquiesce to India's objections and prepared another, much more explicit protest note, which was received on 29 August 1983:

> Your reply to our protest note of 21 August 1983 received.
>
> - Your troops have carried out intrusions across LC north of Point NJ 9842 – Karakoram Pass NE 7410. They intruded approximately 25 miles inside our territory in Siachen Glacier, NJ 9797, NK 0689.
>
> - Last year also your troops had intruded into the same area for which protest had been lodged by our government.
>
> This is a serious violation and unless stopped forthwith is likely to disturb the peaceful condition. Therefore, please instruct your troops to remain south of the line Point NJ 9842 – Karakoram Pass NE 7410.[20]

While intrusions and protest notes were common in the disputed areas of Jammu, Kashmir and Ladakh, it was becoming evident to India that this was not a situation that could be readily solved by the normal counterprotests. The Indian Army decided to continue its patrols, and as noted before, the Polar Bear 2 patrol took place in September 1983, after the Pakistani protest notes were duly received and responded too in the usual manner.

However, to India's Northern Command, it was becoming clear that Pakistan's claim over the Siachen Glacier was more serious than the normal claim and counterclaim. To this end, the Indian Army began a detailed evaluation of the situation of the Siachen situation and the concerns of a possible Pakistani attack on the glacier, a fear reinforced by the reports that Pakistan was sending more civilian expeditions to the area and that the Pakistan Army was moving to procure a substantial quantity of high altitude warfare clothing and other equipment necessary for operations in extreme cold weather conditions and heavy snow cover.

Both the Indian Army and the Indian Intelligence Agency – the Research and Analysis Wing (RAW) – began to prepare detailed assessments of the situation. Vikram Sood, former Chief of RAW was, in 1983, the agency's station chief in Srinagar and he was routinely passing on information from the agency to the Army, especially Lt. Gen Prem N. Hoon – Commander of 15 Corps in Srinagar – regarding Pakistani activity:

> That time, we knew Pakistanis were sending more and more civilian expeditions into Siachen, but its importance was not so apparent until we put two and two together and realised Pakistan was up to something far more serious than just sending mountaineering expeditions into the area. When we got reports of the large scale snow clothing and high altitude equipment purchase by Pakistan, there was enough urgency for me to go and share it with Prem (Lt. General Hoon)… The Pakistanis were not buying all that for a picnic.[21]

As part of its preliminary preparations in late 1983, the Indian Army's assessment, based on its own military intelligence plus input from RAW made the following observations prior to Operation Meghdoot:

> We had been launching expeditions and patrols onto the Siachen Glacier since 1978. Pakistan launched protests against our activities in 1983 on the plea that our patrols have intruded into their territory. Their claim to the territory is part of their geostrategic scheme backed by the incorrect and unilateral marking of the imaginary extension of the LC on maps published in the USA. From the various intelligence reports received it was confirmed that Pak[istan] was sending an appropriately equipped force in the area to contest out patrol in 1984.[22]

Hindsight is often correct but it might be argued that a combination of factors – intelligence from RAW, the Indian Army's own assessments, plus the tenor and tone of Pakistan's August 1983 protest notes, gave India the strong impression that Pakistan was planning a military operation on the Siachen Glacier in the very short term. Planning thus commenced for the launch of an Indian operation to pre-empt any such Pakistani move on the glacier. These preparations began in September 1983 after patrol Polar Bear 2 returned from the Siachen Glacier in 1983. These preparations were made in a very comprehensive manner.[23] Lt. General Chibber was to note that: 'Our presence in this area till 1983 had been in the form of expeditions and patrols, which were considered inadequate to meet possible Pakistani reaction. It was, therefore, decided to launch a sizeable force suitably equipped to operate in the Siachen Glacier during 1984.'[24]

Lt. General Chibber, who was closely involved with India's Siachen planning since 1978, was concerned that an Indian operation on the Siachen Glacier, especially one which involved Indian troops occupying Sia La and Bilafond La, could result in a local conflict with Pakistan which could escalate further into a broader conflict, with assessments ranging from a localised clash, to a conflict along the LoC or one which, in the pre-nuclear period in the Indian subcontinent, could result in generalised hostilities across both the LoC and the international border with attendant risks to India, especially given its internal security situation.[25]

However, Lt. General Chibber was adamant that an operation had to be launched and he made sure to include in his assessments that there was a need to launch an operation to occupy the passes on the Saltoro Ridge and detailed the Pakistani intentions and deployment as follows: 'Pakistan had inducted a column consisting of one Cdo Coy [Commando Company] and one NLI [Northern Light Infantry] Coy supported by a mortar pl [platoon] to Sai La. Pakistan's build up of this column was delayed due to the late arrival from abroad of snow clothing and equipment.'[26]

As planning for Operation Meghdoot, which was approved without requiring too much convincing, was in progress, Chibber continued to make telling observations to the Indian Army noting that:

> Whilst we were planning and preparing for *Operation Meghdoot*, there were intelligence reports that indicated Pak[istan] had designs of launching a military operation in the area. Some of the pertinent indicators were as follows:
>
> - *Cancellation of Leave*: In January 1984, it was learnt that turnover of troops/units, as also leave of persons in Force Command Northern Area had been suspended till September 1984.
> - *Laying lines of communication*: In December 1983, intelligence reported laying of line of communications ahead of Skardu. Later in April 1984, reports pertaining to establishment of an exchange at Khapalu were also received.
> - *Procurement of high altitude equipment*: Reports in November 1983 had indicated Pak procuring approximately 1,000 sets of high altitude clothing and other equipment.[27]

As will be discussed later, these observations were not incorrect and Pakistan was already making initial preparations for an operation to pre-empt an Indian intervention in the area. The two countries were each attempting to forestall the other.

Pakistan and India, not unexpectedly, moved towards stationing troops and occupying the Siachen Glacier. Each anticipated that the other would move and as such both armies prepared to get their troops into position as quickly as possible.

On the Pakistani side, Lt. General Jahandad Khan, who was in 1983-84 the Commander of the Rawalpindi based X Corps, following an encounter in September 1983 where a SSG company crossed the Bilafond La Pass and a helicopter caused an Indian Ladakh Scouts patrol to withdraw, wrote:

> The withdrawal of the SSG Company was followed by many meetings in the GHQ to decide our plan of action for the summer of 1984 when the Indians were bound to come in greater numbers. Also taken into consideration was the fact that whoever succeeded in occupying the passes first would be able to hold them as it was impossible to dislodge them from these positions due to the terrain and the conditions. As Corps Commander I gave the following assessment to the GHQ.
>
> Next year, 1984, India is most likely to pre-empt the occupation of the main passes of the Saltoro Ridge with two battalion strength of occupation and a third battalion in reserve. It would need another brigade to provide them with logistics support. Maximum helicopter force will have to be utilized for logistics support. The Air Force will be able for air cover and also air drop of supplies and equipment.
>
> We will need a brigade group with a battalion plus to occupy these passes and the rest of the force to provide relief and logistics support. We would also need maximum porter force to carry supplies and ammunition from Goma to the glacier positions. All our helicopter force, both Alouette and Puma will have to be mobilized for reconnaissance and logistics cover. PAF has to stand by to provide air cover. I had cautioned GHQ that this operation will be very costly in logistics support. Our military intelligence must be alerted to keep us informed of all enemy movements beyond Leh to forestall their occupation of the glacier area.[28]

From this remarkably prescient appreciation, Pakistan thus decided to establish a permanent piquet at Siachen. The Pakistani GHQ, under the chairmanship of the President and dictator of Pakistan, Zia-ul-Haq, considered the issue and once again were very prescient in their appreciation that the Indians could deploy and sustain perhaps a brigade as opposed to a battalion from Pakistan.[29] Lt. General Khan continued:

> In this meeting it was decided to incorporate the PAF in this operation and Major General Pir Dad Khan (Commander of the Northern Areas) was given the task of pre-empting the occupation of the passes, reaching there not before May 1984, as weather conditions before that period would not allow the use of helicopters and the PAF. This decision was to be approved by the Defence Coordination Committee (DCC), attended by the Joint Staffs Committee and all service chiefs. So preparatory work was started on procurement of high altitude equipment and clothing, improvement of roads and tracks, recruitment of porters etc. All these preparations were to be completed by April 1984.
>
> I handed over command of 10 Corps to Lt. General Zahid Ali Akbar Khan on 31 March 1984 after completing my tenure of four years. I gave him a detailed briefing about this operational plan and particularly stressed the importance of intelligence keeping a watch on Indian moves beyond Leh. However, I learned later that when our troops approached the Saltoro Ridge passes during the third week of May 1984, the Indians were already in occupation of Gyong Pass in the south, strategically important because it could interfere with the enemy's line of logistics support. As it was impossible to dislodge the Indians, we had no option but to occupy the next highest feature opposite them. This was a great setback for Pakistan, although all plans, including the timing of the troop movement, had been laid down at the highest level. We had obviously failed to detect the movement of a brigade size force in the area. It was learnt that the Indians had moved up their troops from Leh in the second half of April 1984.
>
> After the occupation of these positions by both sides, opposite each other, the border became active. Both sides started inducting heavy weapons including artillery guns, rocket launchers and anti-aircraft missiles. Fire duels, patrol clashes and engagement of helicopters through anti-aircraft guns became a daily affair. Both sides also brought up more troops to counter each other. Since then, there has been no substantial change in the relative positions on both sides. It was in the winter of 1984 that the Pakistani troops first experienced operating at that altitude. But the troops were provided high altitude equipment and there was no abnormal loss of life due to weather conditions.[30]

As can be seen, Pakistan had an excellent appreciation as to what India's intentions might be in respect of deploying troops to the Siachen Glacier. They had carefully planned an operation to seize the initiative in anticipation of India's move and had prepared troops, logistics and air support to sustain an operation to take control of the Glacier and the Saltoro Ridge. It was countered by an audacious Indian military operation which involved very much the same type of appreciation of Pakistan's intentions and possible plans to take the Siachen Glacier. In a strange way, but characteristic of two professional military forces, both the Indian and Pakistani armies anticipated, appreciated and understood the military objectives that the other would follow in moving towards military operations on the Siachen Glacier. However, in India, the planning took place in somewhat more detail and started at an earlier date. In so doing, India was able to gain a crucial time advantage over Pakistan and was able to secure its objectives and entrench itself accordingly.

Preparations for Operation Meghdoot

India's preparations for its assault on the Siachen Glacier were moved into earnest in January 1984. The Indian Army's Northern Command, in particular its XV Corps were working towards preparing assault teams to reach the Saltoro Ridge, the watershed west of the Siachen Glacier. There was an emphasis on occupying Indira Col, Sia La and Bilafond La, which were the most prominent passes on the Saltoro Ridge as soon as possible. Once the planning was in progress, Lt. General Chibber wrote to the then Chief of Army Staff, General A.S. Vaidya, in January 1984 to seek formal approval for the operations.[31]

As part of the planning, 79 Brigade Group which was part of XV Corps was to be designated as the 'Himalayan Brigade' for operations in extreme snow conditions. The plan was for this force to be equipped to a very high standard with specialised high altitude and cold weather gear plus special ski equipment.[32] It was proposed that this brigade group was to be equipped to the same standard as the assault force that would stage Operation Meghdoot. In the event, this did not happen in quite the way envisaged and 102 Infantry Brigade was selected instead. Northern Command in its note on the subject to General Vaidya stated, seeking as India's Northern Command did to cover all eventualities in its planning:

> Besides organizing and tailoring a specialised task force, it is essential to provide it a dedicated helicopter unit equipped with Mi-8 and Cheetah helicopters. Fire support from armed helicopters and air photos for areas of interest is also recommended. Logistics infrastructure in the form of air maintenance and road communications from Sasoma to Base Camp, construction of helipads at the Base Cam and Sasoma and construction of fibre glass shelters is also planned.[33]

This note was followed by detailed discussions with General Vaidya as well as the Director General of Military Operations Lt. General A.S. Somanna, on 9 February 1984. Five days later, full planning for Operation Megdoot began in earnest. This included determining which formations were to be deployed, identifying the officers to lead the assault as well as the supporting formations to be employed to assist and to be ready to reinforce the initial units deployed to seize and secure the Siachen Glacier and the Saltoro Ridge. The major decisions regarding these key issues were taken on 14 February.[34]

Northern Command assigned one company plus one platoon of the Ladakh Scouts, a formation recruited from the people of Ladakh and which was initially a paramilitary force assigned to work with the Indian Army following the war with China, to be part of supporting the assault. The Ladakh Scouts were to emerge as a highly capable and decorated unit in conflicts post-1963 and were to become a full regiment of the Indian Army in 1999 after their stellar performance in the Kargil War. In 1984, however, they were a small, capable unit that was to play an important role during operations. Other than this company plus one platoon of the Ladakh Scouts, the other unit assigned to supporting the assault on the Siachen Glacier was a single platoon of the 4 Kumaon.[35] This does not seem to be an overly generous force level for the operation envisaged but it is completely in accordance with the difficulty of supporting any sizeable force at that altitude and that too for the first time. The limits of logistics, air support and the ability of troops to operate at extreme altitudes and extremely low temperatures would be tested to the limit.

The actual assault forces were under the overall command of Lt Colonel Pushkar Chand, the Commanding Officer of 1 Vikas Battalion of the Special Frontier Force. He was to establish his command post at the Forward Logistics Base at an altitude of 16,000 feet. An additional company of 19 Kumaon, under its own Commanding Officer, Lt. Colonel Khanna, was prepared to aid 1 Vikas in the event of any military or emergency contingency arising.[36] This company was located at Sasoma and, following its feats at Gorichen, was an experienced unit and well capable of operating at very high altitudes.

What might be rather surprising, as the Indian troops began to train and equip themselves for this operation, Army HQ, through letter No. A/35501/XM03 of 31 March 1983 defined the Indian Army's objectives in extremely limited terms and it is apparent that a major offensive operation to take and hold the Siachen Glacier. The letter listed the tasks as follows:

- Tasks in General: Secure the Siachen Glacier
- Tasks in Particular: Secure Bilafond La, Sia La, Siachen, Lolofond and Teram Sehar Glacier
- Patrol up to Indira Col
- Prevent Pakistan Sponsored Infiltration in the area.[37]

The Army HQ directive would seem to indicate that operations were aimed at deploying troops to hold the Saltoro Ridge, especially its heights. Even then-Prime Minister Indira Gandhi did not seem to be keen on a broader or sustained deployment and her own directive was a simple order to secure the Siachen Glacier. With India's very precarious internal security situation, with insurgencies in the north-eastern states of Nagaland, Manipur and Mizoram and terrorism becoming a major challenge in Punjab, the Indian government was very wary about committing any significant resources to the campaign for the glacier.

The Siachen task force was moved to Sasoma on 28 March 1984 and the Indian Air Force began to airlift stores and other supplies. Some 461 tonnes were airlifted between 19 March 1984 and August 1984. Infrastructure was prepared at the base camp with high altitude huts being constructed as well as a helipad for Mi-8 helicopters. These would lift stores to the base camp and thereafter Cheetahs would move stores from Sasoma to the Forward Logistics Base and from the base camp to the assault camp. The only shortcoming in the schedule was the snow clothing for the assault teams for Bilafond La and Sia La.[38]

The Path to Siachen and Operation Meghdoot

The supporting force comprising 19 Kumaon began to move on 18 March 1984. The full strength of the battalion, 14 Officers, 20 Junior Commissioned Officers and 473 Other Ranks, after a prayer at the Mandir of the unit's patron Goddess – Kalika Mata – began its 630 kilometres trek to the Siachen Glacier in its unit transport, augmented by additional three-ton trucks which were there to move the additional supplies needed for the battalion's part in the Siachen operations from its base in Khrew to Siachen.[39]

One other detachment of 19 Kumaon was dispatched by air as an advanced party. This group, of roughly platoon strength, was led by Captain Ajit Samuel and comprised 4 Junior Commissioned Officers and 24 Other Ranks. This detachment was tasked to proceed via transport aircraft – rather surprisingly a C-119 Packet of the IAF – to Leh and Thoise. On the same day the rest of the battalion began is road trek from Khrew. This combination of road and air transport enabled the battalion to get into position in a relatively short period of time given the environment.[40] The fact that a full battalion, its support equipment, plus adequate supplies was able to accomplish this feat in a modest time frame, in extremely hostile conditions with the weather – both cold and extreme snow – being a great obstacle, is testimony to sound planning but also determination and initiative.

Captain Samuel, as Advance Party Commander, was also responsible for inducting, via transport aircraft, all the heavy baggage of the battalion. He described his experience as follows:

> A few days prior to the move, all the companies and the Battalion Headquarters were ordered to prepare their loads for air induction as per the battalion's mobilization scheme, as if it was a mobilization practice. Every small little item was weighed and carefully packed. We were authorized to carry only nine tons of loads by air. On 18 March 1984, the same day the Battalion started its move, the air column under me also left for Thoise in a 'Packet' aircraft and was there in an hour's time. The induction was very smooth. My party comprised of, apart from me, 4 JCOs and 24 other ranks.[41]

On 30 March 1984, 19 Kumaon concentrated at the Leh Transit camp for its onward push. Attempts were made by two companies under Major S.C. Thakur, to cross Khardung La. However, the road was closed and the parties had to return to Leh. To the credit of Major Thakur and his personnel, they repeated their attempts and finally crossed Khardung La on foot and arrived at Khalsar on the bank of the Shyok River on 8 April 1984. Gradually, the other companies and units of the battalion were brought up, consolidating their positions and even bringing along a troop of a light artillery regiment with mortars but at substantially reduced personnel strength. All units were finally in position on 18 April 1984 when the last column under Major D.L. Julka arrived at Sasoma, which allowed an exhausted battalion to finally avail itself of a hot meal, having eaten nothing but haversack rations for their arduous 630 kilometres move from Khrew.[42]

As a fully operational unit, the battalion brought with it all its support equipment, including its mortar platoon under the command of Captain Samir Ganguly. As the operation depended heavily on the determination and capabilities of junior officers, this platoon was to prove to be decisive in ensuring that the 19 Kumaon was able to meet its objectives and get to Sasoma by 18 April 1984. The young officer described his experience as trailblazer in the following terms:

> I was the Mortar Platoon Commander. I trained my Platoon very well and fully motivated them. The Mortar Platoon was nominated to beat the track in heavy snow and white out conditions during the crossing of the Zojila Pass. Although at the time, I thought the decision to put Mortar Platoon to beat the track was wrong, instead an Infantry Platoon should have been detailed, I decided to do the task and lead the Platoon from the front. I put tough boys ahead long with me, distributing the mortar parts to others and I personally carried the bipod of the mortar. This probably came to the notice of the Commanding Officer, Lt. Colonel D.K. Khanna, who had by then reached the Sector HQ. He personally came to North Pulu to receive the Platoon after our crossing of the Khardung La pass and commended the Platoon for their commendable job. I was personally present with the Platoon. It was one of my proudest moments ever.[43]

India's assault on the Siachen Glacier was, as noted, a deliberate plan to drop two platoons – one at Bilafond La and another at Sia La – by Mi-8 and Cheetah helicopters in several sorties. The Indians noted that Pakistan's Puma helicopters could not operate at an altitude high enough to comfortably cross the Saltoro Ridge with any useful load of stores or personnel and as such, even if the Pakistanis were able to get to the Saltoro Ridge Line, by dint of its own considerable initiative and capabilities, it would not be able to sustain its presence there in any way.

Brigadier Channa, selected Captain Sanjay Kulkarni to lead a platoon of 4 Kumaon to Bilafond La thus commencing Operation Meghdoot. Major A.N. Bahuguna was tasked with leading the Ladakh Scouts in platoon strength to take Sia La. As with 19 Kumaon, these troops began to concentrate at Sasoma. On 11 April 1984, 19 Kumaon, concentrated at Leh and a special ski troop force was assembled, comprising five officers, six JCOs and 43 other ranks from HAWS. This attachment of HAWS personnel was to enable the team to overcome any difficulties involved in crossing a snow-bound landscape and was to be invaluable.[44]

Given the numbers of troops involved, helicopter support was adequate but not generous. For medium-lift operations, two Mi-8 helicopters under the command of Wing Commander K.K. Sangar were positioned at Thoise, while a larger force of six smaller Cheetah helicopters which were far better at high altitude operations were placed under the command of Wing Commander G.S. Sandhu. At this stage, the helicopters were not armed though India was quite prepared to deploy weapons aboard its helicopters – rockets and machine guns aboard the Mi-8s and machine guns aboard the Cheetahs – if necessary.[45]

Weapons support was not altogether lavish and rather surprisingly, there was a heavy air defence component. While limited artillery support was provided by four Grad-P single round rocket launchers – a single round launcher using 122mm rockets similar to those used by the Grad multi-barrel rocket launcher – a detachment of two ZU-23-2 guns from 126 Light AD Regiment (Composite) and three detachments of SA-7 Strela-2M man-portable SAMs from 502 AD Group (SP) were positioned at the base camp. Additional anti-aircraft artillery support was available – ZU-23-2 guns – from the rest of 126 Light AD Regiment and 127 Light AD Regiment (Composite).[46] In addition, 105 AD regiment, with radar directed 40mm Bofors L40/70 guns was inducted in September 1984 for the defence of the Base Camp Siachen. This unit became the only AD unit with radar directed guns to cross the Khardung La pass at an altitude of 18,300 feet.[47] From these deployments it is clear that India was concerned about the combination of Pakistani helicopter interference plus the possibility of an air attack on its base camp and other vital areas and points in the Siachen theatre.

The Indian Army began to have discussions on a possible D-Day and H-Hour for the commencement of operations. Northern Command had set a timeframe of between 10 and 30 April 1984. As has been seen, 19 Kumaon was fully in position by early to mid-April 1984. The final date for operations was at the discretion of the Sector Commander, Brigadier Channa. He decided on the date of 13

Amid the surreal landscape of Siachen, infantry movement was always a struggle through deep snow drifts in numbing cold. (Indian Army)

Air Officer Commanding of Jammu and Kashmir and Major General Shiv Sharma all visited the base camp and carried out an aerial survey of Sia La and Bilafond La.[50]

Operation Meghdoot is Launched

Weather conditions on 13 April 1984 were appalling with a snow storm in progress. Yet at 05.30hrs on 13 April 1984, the first Cheetah helicopter sortie was launched, carrying Captain Sanjay Kulkarni of 4 Kumaon and one soldier. This was followed by two more helicopters in succession. By 12.00hrs, 17 sorties had been flown by Squadron Leader Surinder S. Bains and Rohit Rai and had managed to place Captain Kulkarni, one JCO and 27 other ranks at Bilafond La. Captain Kulkarni, who was to retire as a Lt. General, recalled:

> Four of us jumped one by one as the first two helicopters hovered just short of Bila [Bilafond La] around 6.00hrs that day. I remember throwing a 25kg *atta bori* [a gunny sack full of flour] to test the depth and hardness of the snow. It was quite hard. We jumped and then constructed a helipad of sorts to allow the latter sorties to land of half a minute or so and then return for another trip...
>
> The most abiding memory of that day is of course of extreme cold. It must have been minus 30 degrees Celsius. We were to be deployed by 'vertical envelopment' [heli-dropped] at Bilafond La and another platoon led by Major Bahuguna was to be dripped at Sia La, but they couldn't be sent until 17-18 April, because the weather turned bad and remained bad for the next three days. Extremely bad weather.
>
> Within three hours of landing, we had to evacuate our radio operator, one sepoy Mandal, who suffered HAPE [High Altitude Pulmonary Edema (or Oedema)] despite being trained, acclimatized and being fit. So, we had a radio but no radio operator. Of course, it helped since we were supposed to maintain radio silence. So now 28 of us remained at Bilafond La. Within 48 hours we were down to 27. Another boy died in two days. April, after all is winter on Siachen. Of this lot, 21 of us, I remember, got severe frost bites.
>
> All this despite the fact that all these boys had come to me to the glacier in 1983 and were very familiar with the precautions that needed to be taken on the glacier. And this despite the fact that Lt. General Hoon had managed to get us imported snow clothing from abroad, just in the nick of time. I remember they arrived on the evening of 12 April, barely hours we were being launched into *Operation Meghdoot*. Thermal coats, thermal pants, very nice balaclavas, excellent tents, ice axes, goggles, the works were brought from Europe. The weapons, however, remained the basic Indian Army 7.62 mm SLR. Of course, we had mortars, MMG, missiles, Grad P rockets. Some of the weapons came by air, some came through porters. I remember that times they were

April. Brigadier Channa's command style was viewed in some circles as unconventional and he used this in his planning and choice of a date for commencement. His choice was to be an inspired one.[48] In his own words he said:

> Well, what I say may sound controversial, but the fact is that both, the Pakistani Army and us, follow the legacy left behind by the British. When the British planned, they used to be very cautious in their approach, very slow, erring on the side of caution. They were not prone to take risks. But, in such an operation I had to take a risk. And go up when they [the Pakistanis] least expected it. I was proved right.
>
> If you read General [Pervez] Musharraf's book, he says India pre-empted us. What does that indicate? That they [the Pakistanis] were preparing to occupy those passes too. I also know that when our team went abroad to buy snow clothing, the Pakistanis were already doing so; when we were collecting quotations, they had already brought snow suits outright!
>
> So it was a race against time. You see the operating season on the glacier is generally end-May/early June when they say it is comparatively safe to operate. So, one had to choose that time frame. Pakistanis had a much shorter problem, had lesser logistical problems. I would say no more. It was one of those intuitions where I said let's do it early. I was asked about it. When would I like to launch? I mulled over it and thought about *Baisakhi* (a harvest festival observed with much fanfare in North India, and even in Pakistani Punjab). Now, *Baisakhi* is celebrated with equal fervour on both sides. People are in a joyous mood. Their guard is down. It was also the most unlikely date to launch a military operation. So there you are. 13 April it was. I would concede it was risky. Some called it suicidal. But that's exactly why we had to do it that day. Rest is history![49]

With this bizarre, but in retrospect entirely sensible reasoning, Northern Command was informed of Brigadier Channa's choice and as such, the date for the commencement of military operations was set. Reconnaissance of the area of intended operations was undertaken by senior officers with the commander of Western Air Command, Air Marshal MSO Wollen, Air Vice Marshal A Dayala,

A Cheetah helicopter of the Indian Army Aviation Corps seen landing on one of the elevated platforms necessary to enable safe landings on mountain sides. (Albert Grandolini Collection)

Indian Army troops seen during the advance of April 1984. (Indian Army)

getting 50 rupees per porter per day, almost equivalent to the porter fee for expeditions to Mount Everest. But we didn't mind since they were all local Ladakhis.[51]

It was then that the weather took a devastating turn for the worse, placing at risk Captain Kulkarni and his surviving soldiers. While at Bilafond La, the weather 'packed up', visibility fell to zero and this had the effect of immediately grounding the fragile fleet of Cheetahs. Future sorties were thus ruled out. Kulkarni recalled: 'The blizzard hit us even as the two-man pup tents were being set up. It was damn difficult. At that point of time, the higher authorities must have thought that this was a big mistake. We remained out of contact for three days.'[52] Yet, among all that confusion, inclement weather and despite the casualties already suffered to the environment, the Indian flag was planted on Bilafond La on 13 April 1984.

Despite this initial success, the bad weather and loss of contact with Captain Kulkarni's team started a certain amount of recrimination. The Staff at Northern Command and the Military Operations Directorate were worried as the plan to send troops to the Siachen Glacier in winter seemed to be condemning good men to almost certain death. There was perhaps understandable fear of displeasure from higher authorities.

Brigadier Channa, as the person who took the final decision to send Captain Kulkarni and his troops to Bilafond La on 13 April 1984, found himself cautiously confident:

There were many who stared at me with the 'I told you so' look. But to be frank, I was still confident that the storm would pass over. And it did. Three days later. The radio silence worked wonderfully. The Pakis came to know about the operation only after we had established and occupied the post at Bilafond La, that too because Sanjay opened the radio to tell us that one boy had died of hypoxia.[53]

Even while Captain Kulkarni's team remained out of contact, the ground troops began their inexorable, arduous move on foot from the base camp and established Camp II on 13 April 1984. Along the route to Bilafond La, Camp II and Camp III were established by 15 April. Lt. Colonel Pushkar Chand, Task Force Commander moved the Ladakh Scouts and 19 Kumaon units to Camp I and thereafter to Camp II. Pushkar Chand, to maintain morale, contact and experience the terrain, walked to every post he established during his six-month duty tenure.[54]

After a three-day period of great tension, the weather improved on 17 April 1984. The Indian Air Force prepared to conduct its operations and was able on that day to fly 32 helicopters using all available serviceable assets. Both Mi-8s were operational and pressed into service. However, only five of the six Cheetahs were available on that day but they too worked to reinforce and resupply the Bilafond La position with supplies, equipment and replacement personnel. This air lift was instrumental in those early days in securing India's precarious hold on this most important part of the Siachen Glacier.[55]

On that same day, Major Ajay Bahuguna and his platoon of Ladakh Scouts were able to reach and occupy Sia La. In this case, the helicopters had to drop Major Bahuguna and his troops some five kilometres east of Sia La. To reach their objective, the Ladakh Scouts, even accustomed to the terrain of Ladakh which is inhospitable at

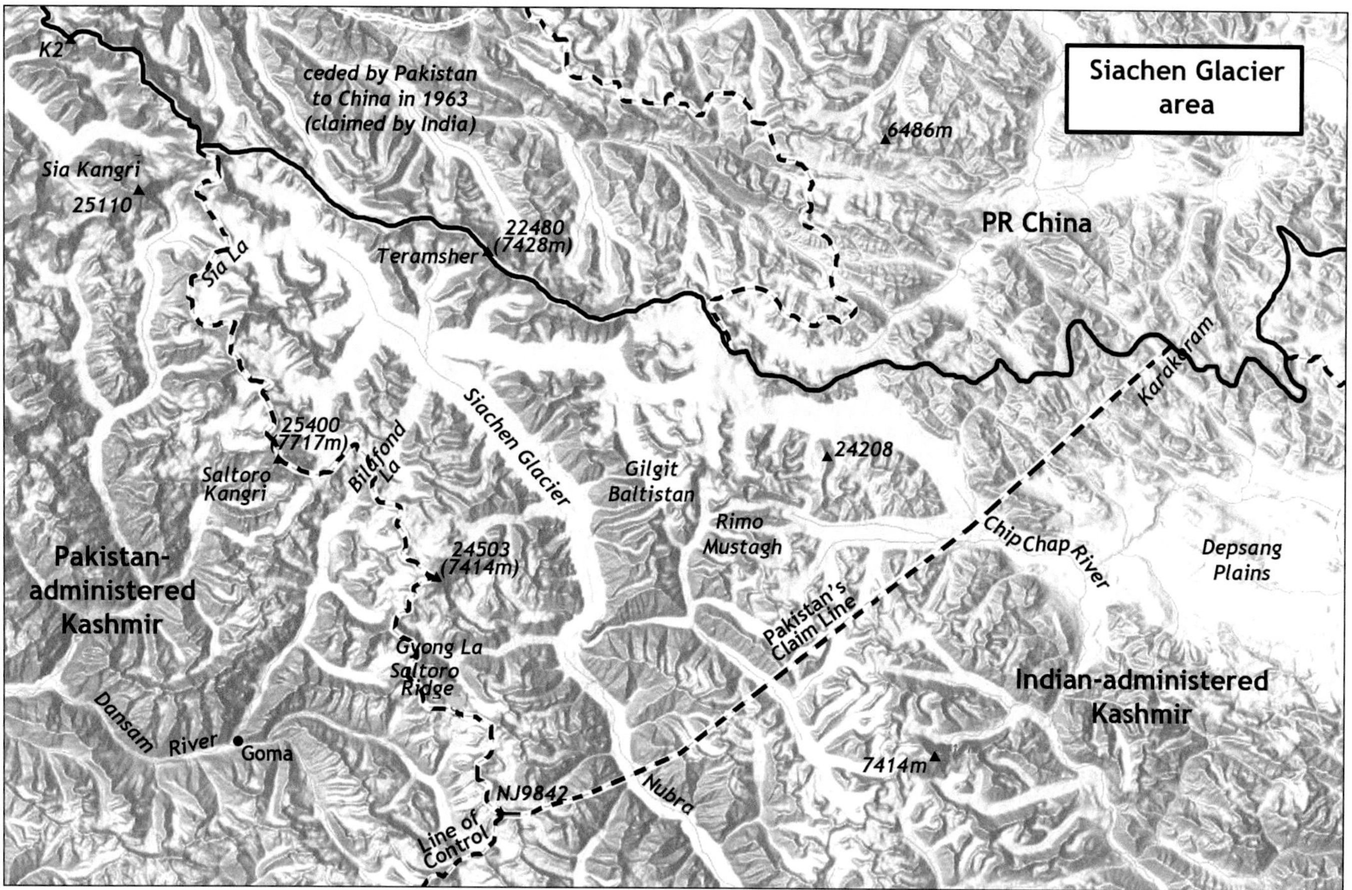

Map of the Siachen Glacier area since 1984. (Map by Tom Cooper)

best, had to scale difficult slopes and compounded by the very heavy snowfall over the preceding days, made movement a slow, deliberate and extremely dangerous affair. Yet, the Ladakh Scouts were able to meet their objective and in good time.[56]

At this time, as Captain Kulkarni broke radio silence to announce the death of one of his men, a Pakistani helicopter overflew Bilafond La. Kulkarni says: "When the Pakistanis saw us, they turned. If they had not seen us, they would have probably done exactly the same thing (heli dropped at Bilafond La). Now they had no chance. They realised we were already at Bilafond La!"[57]

India speeded up the construction of infrastructure and connectivity at this time. The link up force established the Forward Logistics Base (FLB) in the basic area of the Siachen Glacier on 18 April and Camp IV on 22 April. The link up with Bilafond La post took place on 24 August. On the same day, Camp V was created. Following the creation of Camp VI on 26 April, the remaining Indian forces were divided into two parties. One party established the assault camp at Indira Col and Turkestan La on 29 April. The other party, commanded by Major N. S. Salaria of the Ladakh Scouts was able to link up with the Sia La post on the same day.[58] This completed the initial stage of Operation Meghdoot which achieved its objectives in a spectacular fashion at relatively low cost.

Pakistan's Counterstroke – Preparations for Operation Ababeel

Pakistan was very surprised by India's seizure of the Siachen Glacier and Saltoro Ridge and began its countermove. As noted earlier, its own assault on the glacier, codenamed Operation Ababeel had been planned and war gamed since January 1984. The initial plan was to go through the passes of Bilafond La and Sia La, however, with these in Indian hands, the plans shifted to other routes of ingress along

The Pakistani operation began with the deployment of reinforcements and their equipment from low elevations to forward operating bases near the conflict zone. Due to the lack of roads, nearly everything had to be carried by helicopters. This photograph shows a Pakistan Army Puma carrying a light artillery piece. (Albert Grandolini Collection)

An Alouette III landing at one of the Pakistani forward operating bases at lower altitude, near the Siachen Glacier. (Albert Grandolini Collection)

the Saltoro Ridge. To this end, the Pakistan Army began to gather a special unit, with its SSG to respond to India.

The formation of the Pakistani Burzil Force of the sector controlled by 80 Brigade was surprising because the Siachen Glacier came under the control of 62 Brigade. A headquarters was prepared at Khapalu for controlling Operation Ababeel. The preparations were noticed by India's Northern Command by 15 May through extensive use of aerial reconnaissance and other intelligence means, who were then able to prepare a detailed appreciation of the Pakistani plans, and the objectives of the Pakistani counterstroke.[59] To this end, Northern Command was able to prepare a detailed note outlining the Pakistani plans and possible forces as well as its objectives:

> In our appreciation, Pak had formed several task forces to try and wrest back control from India. These were:
>
> - Hyder Force: Approximately one company minus of SSG [Special Services Group] and one section of NLI [Northern Light Infantry] at location NJ 6299, approximately 10 kilometres south-west of Sia La.
> - Baber Force: One company of SSG and one platoon of NLI located in Ali Bransa.
> - Ashgar Force: The force comprising one company of SSG and one platoon of NLI was operating on the Chumik Glacier and also patrolling towards the Gyongla glacier at point NK 0069.
> - Hafeez Force: This force of approximately one company was probably operating between the Hyder and Baber forces with the view of exploiting any gaps/ unoccupied dominating heights.

The closer to Siachen the Pakistanis moved, the higher the altitude became and thus the lighter the involved helicopters. Closest to the combat zone it was exclusively the light Lamas of the Army Aviation Corps that were deployed. (Albert Grandolini Collection)

Pakistan Army troops underway in the snow at lower elevations in the Siachen Glacier in the mid-1980s. (Albert Grandolini Collection)

- Kalander Force: This force, probably trained for infiltration tasks, was inducted in the area in the first week of May 1984, to probably disrupt Indian lines of communications. However, detailed movement/ deployment of this force could not be known.
- Our analysis showed that while SSG soldiers were being used for occupation of defences, NLI troops were used for administration duties, occupation of base camps, and to act as reserves or to be deployed for route opening and as combat porters.
- By the first week of May 1984, Pakistan build up opposite our glacial poss and in the area of Gyong La had increased considerably. There were also intelligence reports of Pakistan's likely intentions to infiltrate through the gap between the Kargil and Gallies sectors. Our forward troops in this area also reported reinforcement of some Pakistan posts opposite the Kargil sector.[60]

An early forward operating bases of the Indian Army on the Siachen Glacier. (Indian Army)

The interior of an Indian Army bunker in the Siachen area: in the foreground is a Browning M2HB 12.7mm heavy machine gun mounted on a tripod. Note the canisters, sacks and barrels – all certainly filled with sand and gravel, covered with snow and ice even inside the position. (Indian Army)

As can be seen, Pakistan had made strenuous efforts to train, equip and build up a sufficient level of forces to pose a serious threat to India's positions on the Siachen Glacier. In light of this advanced warning, India moved to prepare itself as best it could for the inevitable Pakistani counterstroke. However, despite being forewarned, India was faced with serious difficulties in establishing sufficient surveillance to prevent its positions from being compromised by Pakistani troops. Terrain, weather and the physical difficulties of the environment all were against easy preparations but India managed to bring both firepower and personnel into position.

India's Build Up in Response

Northern Command and 15 Corps were both aware that Pakistan had to be stopped from gaining access across the Saltoro Ridge to the Siachen Glacier. Bilafond La and Sia La were under Indian control, and as such, Pakistan sought to use the path across the watershed of Gyong La. General Chibber conducted a visit of the Indian area of operations on 22 April 1984 and after extensive aerial surveys, he gave the following orders:

While climbing up the sides of the Siachen Glacier was always an arduous task, going downhill was frequently much simpler, as demonstrated by this group of Pakistani troops. (Albert Grandolini Collection)

- Patrolling of all southern glaciers, that is Gyong La, Langongma, Layogma, Urdolep and Korisa to be carried out by our troops to counter infiltration attempts.
- Enemy will be prevented from establishing any hold on the Saltoro range or areas east of it.
- Patrolling of Teram Sehar glacier to be undertaken immediately.[61]

With these directives having been given, Lt General Hoon issued orders to hasten the movement of Indian troops to the Saltoro crest line, in particular to Gyong La. He gave orders that the back-up platoons were to be moved to the passes at Sia La and Bilafond La with a view to dominating the heights and to conduct regular patrolling. Lt. Colonel Pushkar Chand moved to the Forward Logistics Base and received reinforcements in the form of a platoon from each of the Ladakh Scouts and 19 Kumaon. Major Sujan Singh, as Officer in Charge, Ladakh Scouts (Karakoram Wing) was given the responsibility of establishing and organising a base camp with two companies from 19 Kumaon and one platoon of the Ladakh Scouts. He was also tasked with moving stores from the base camp to Camps I, II and III. At this point, one company from 19 Kumaon was ordered to move to Gyong La and take and hold the crest line. This, it was hoped would forestall any Pakistani advances in the area and at the very least, provide sufficient forces to delay any sustained Pakistani action until reinforcements could be sent to the area or support provided.

One company of 19 Kumaon under Lt. Colonel Khanna advanced towards the crest line of Gyong La but their progress was extremely slow and even after 14 days of marching from the base camp, the company was still moving towards the crest line in the general area of the administrative base. Brigadier Channa, during an aerial survey, noticed Pakistani troops around Saddle 6646, indicating that they had secured a foothold at that point.

He therefore ordered Lt. Colonel Khanna to move towards the crest line as soon as possible and to engage the Pakistanis by manoeuvring his troops to a suitable position of advantage or, failing that, by physical action. After an 18-day march across difficult terrain, the company of 19 Kumaon finally reached the crest line. By the first week of June 1984, a company of 19 Kumaon was consolidated and in position on Gyong La. They also occupied Point 5705, OP Hill, the Ring Contour and the eastern slopes of Point 5965, thus bringing the areas south and west of the crest line under Indian control, though with great difficulty.[62] As a Northern Command communication of that period was to note:

> Our maintenance route to Point 5705 la over very difficult and a crevassed surface. To overcome this problem, troops of 1 Vikas were ordered to open a route through Zingrulma glacier. Namgyal Sangpo gallantly led his boys through a very treacherous route, negotiating a large number of crevasses and a few ice walls. This party constructed a helipad at Point 5615 NL 7145. From this helipad, we were able to 'manpack' a M18 57mm recoilless rifle to Point 5705, to engage well entrenched enemy positions built into the rock face at OP II.[63]

Efforts were also made to enhance the patrolling and deployment of the southern glaciers in the area – namely Langogma, Lyogma, Urdolep and Korisa. In addition, efforts were made to get onto the watershed. This was not possible, at least not in all places, owing to a combination of exceedingly difficult terrain plus the ice walls. However, through these sustained efforts, India had established a presence sufficient to ensure close surveillance of the glacier. In addition, ski troopers were drafted from HAWS and they patrolled up to Indira Col and Turkestan La to establish surveillance of the approaches to Siachen from the north.[64]

Conditions were terrible and keeping on alert was a challenge with the ever-present threat of a Pakistani response. Sanjay Kulkarni, whose platoon had been on Bilafond La since 13 April, described the situation prior to the start of Operation Ababeel:

> Although the Pakistanis had spotted us immediately after we got deployed in mid-April, they did not open fire until 25 April. The fire wasn't effective simply because they were firing from a lower altitude. But we had to be ever vigilant. We couldn't allow them to climb up to the pass [Bilafond La]. So there were zero margins for error. Therefore, I had posted one sentry at the very edge of the pass, about 500 metres from where our tents were pitched. The [listening post] sentry would stand at the farthest point possible to look out for any Pakistani troop movement from below. From that position the sentry could see at least a km into Pakistan territory. It was monotonous and physically very demanding task in the cold and blizzards. But it had to be done.
>
> We had put in place a system where every hour the sentry would come and give a report and I would respond by saying 'Okay' or 'Ram Ram' or 'all right'. I used to have a lantern on in

Designed by the Armament Research and Development Establishment (ARDE) of India, in 1972, the Light Field Gun is a towed variant of the British-designed L13 105mm howitzer that was installed in the self-propelled FV433 Abbot. Thanks to its compactness, the capability to elevate the gun up to 70 degrees, a range of up to 17.4km, and a rate of fire of between 6 and 8 shells per minute, it proved highly popular in service. The LFG quickly proved superior to such Soviet-made artillery pieces as the 122mm D-30 howitzer or the 130mm M-46 gun, even though it fired much lighter shells that caused slightly less damage. Thanks to its ruggedness, and ability to be transported by helicopter, the Indian Light Field Gun is nowadays one of the most-widely used artillery pieces of the Indian Army's mountain formations. (Artwork by Anderson Subtil)

The OTO Melara Mod 56 is an Italian-made 105mm howitzer, developed in the late 1950s to meet a requirement for a modern, lightweight howitzer to be used by the Italian Army's Alpini units. Pakistan is known to have purchased 113 of these in the 1970s, not only because of the weapon's high quality, but also because it weighs only 1,290kg and can be disassembled into 12 man-portable parts. These qualities enable it to be transported in a number of ways – including by troops, by mules or by light helicopters. While this light weight could also prove a drawback, because the M56 thus lacked the robustness necessary for sustained operations, in combat the weapon has proved perfectly capable of being deployed in the direct fire role. Designed for mountain warfare, its gun can be elevated up to 65 degrees in the vertical axis: though when deployed inside the narrow gorges of the Siachen area, which are surrounded by very high peaks, this is sometimes a disadvantage. Depending on ammunition, the M56's maximum range is up to 10,000m, and a well-trained crew can reach a rate of fire of up to 10 rounds per minute. More recently, the Chinese corporation NORINCO has manufactured its own version of the M56 and associated ammunition, and it is perfectly possible that the Pakistan Army has sourced additional examples from the People's Republic of China. (Artwork by Anderson Subtil)

This illustration shows an anti-aircraft gunner of the Ladakh Scouts; a regiment of the Indian Army staffed primarily by members of local ethnic groups. He is shown wearing a winter parka over the uniform in Indian Disruptive Pattern Material (not related to the British design with the same designation). His snow glasses and wool hat are standard issue, as is his primary weapon: the Russian-made 9K32M Strela-2M (ASCC/NATO-codename 'SA-7b Grail') short-range, infra-red-homing, shoulder-launched missile (or MANPAD). (Artwork by Anderson Subtil)

This machine gunner of the Pakistan Army is shown wearing the standard woollen blouse, typical of that nation's army uniform, and the no less traditional British-style, canvas-belt. His clothing for the extremely cold weather was primarily sourced from Great Britain, and includes padded pants, snow boots, a commando-style hat and small snow googles. While Pakistan frequently emphasises its good relations with the West, its armed forces make as much use of armament and equipment of Soviet/Russian origin: he is shown operating a 12.7x108mm DShK heavy machine gun of Soviet design, installed on a tripod. (Artwork by Anderson Subtil)

This artillerist of the Pakistan Army is shown as climbing a rock wall. Notable is his heavy camouflage suit in white, standardised alpine leather boots, and his personal weapon – a German made Heckler & Koch G3 assault rifle – which is locally manufactured by the Pakistan Ordnance Works. As usual for both sides, whoever moves up in the direction of Siachen carries additional ammunition and supplies: correspondingly, his backpack is shown containing several 105mm projectiles for the OTO Melara M56 howitzer. (Artwork by Anderson Subtil)

This mountain warfare specialist of the Kumaon Regiment, Indian Army, is shown outfitted for the region's extreme conditions, including a thickly-padded parka and trousers, waterproof leggings and snow boots. His hands are protected by thick gloves and his head is afforded similar protection by a thermal cap. That said, the rest of his gear – including the large backpack and snow glasses – appear to have been purchased on the civilian market: the only 'true military' item is his Indian-made version of the 7.62mm FN FAL assault rifle. (Artwork by Anderson Subtil)

While the slightly bigger HAL Chetak (Aérospatiale SE.316B Alouette III, manufactured under licence in India), serial number Z-1410 of the 114 Helicopter Unit, IAF, was the first helicopter to make a landing on the Siachen Glacier, over the following years it was mainly the lighter and smaller HAL Cheetah (licence-built version of the Aérospatiale SE.315 Alouette II) that saw most action over the highest battlefield in the world. Ultimately, not only was the 114 HU re-equipped with them, but the Indian Army Aviation Corps established two units equipped with Cheetahs: Observation Squadrons 663 and 668. All were painted in dark green overall: air-force-operated examples wore four-digit serials prefixed with Z and applied in black, while Army-operated examples had their markings applied in white, as shown in the inset. (Artwork by Luca Canossa)

By 1984, India had acquired at least 100 Mil Mi-8s, which were locally nicknamed the Rana. Nearly all wore the standardised camouflage pattern shown here, consisting of blue-grey and dark green on upper surfaces and sides. Undersurfaces were initially painted in light grey, but later on this was replaced by the same blue-grey as used higher up. National markings were worn in the form of roundels, applied on the rear and the bottom of the cabin: the national tricolore was always applied on the boom. Serials in the range Z1300-Z1399 (shown is Z1363) were initially worn in black, but later re-applied in the same white as service titles. The rear cargo door was frequently removed for operations over the Siachen area, to lower the weight of the helicopter and thus increase the payload, and also to enable para-drops of supplies and equipment for troops on the ground. (Artwork by Tom Cooper)

Until the acquisition of Mil Mi-17s in the 1990s, the Aérospatiale SA.330 Puma was the principal transport and utility helicopter of the Pakistan Army Aviation Corps. Since 1968, this service and the PAF acquired about 45 Pumas, including about 30 more powerful SA.330Js, equipped with composite rotor blades that enable a higher maximum take-off weight. Thirty remain in service with Nos. 24 and 28 Squadrons. While wearing a standardised camouflage pattern in Brun Café (Sand, FS35189), Brun Noisette (dark red-brown), and Gris Vert Fonce (dark green) on top surfaces and sides, and light grey on undersides, Pakistan Army-operated examples always have the service title applied in white on the boom, and four-digit serials (for example:1415, 1436, 1458, 1522, or 1580) on the nose, and the side of the cabin. The national marking is applied on the rear and the bottom of the cabin. (Artwork by Tom Cooper)

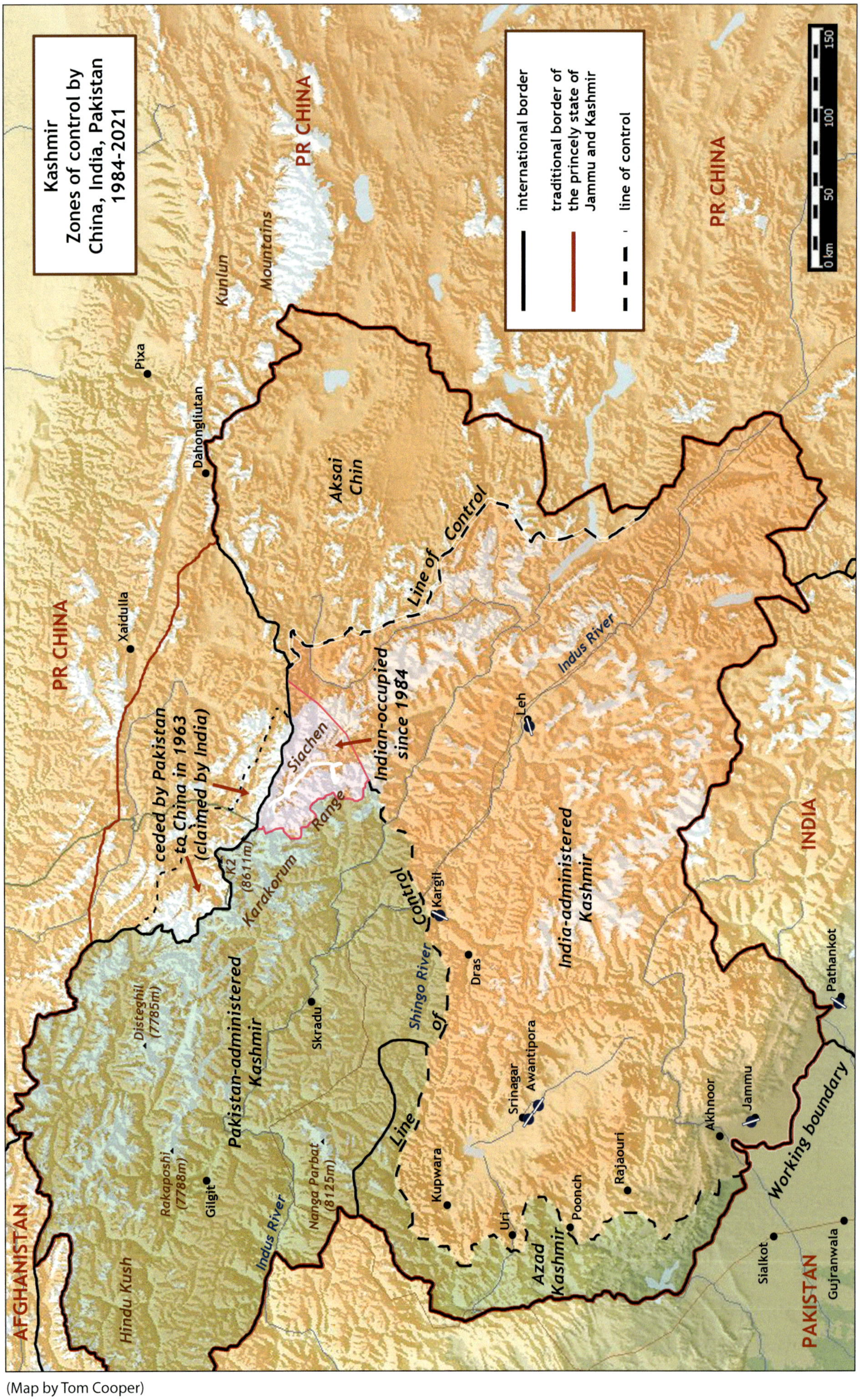

(Map by Tom Cooper)

the tent so that even in the dark, the soldiers would know that this was the Platoon Commander's post. I had told them, if I don't respond, peep into my tent and see if I am dead or alive. For all you know, I could be dead. But, as it is, you sleep less at those altitudes, so I would be mostly awake or semi-awake when they came and gave the report every hour. The system paid rich dividends later.[65]

An OTO Melara M56 pack howitzer of the Pakistan Army in position inside one of the numerous canyons surrounding the Siachen Glacier. (Albert Grandolini Collection)

Another view of a Pakistani-operated M56. Note the heavy wear and soiling of the light coloured alpine uniforms of the crew. (Albert Grandolini Collection)

While India prepared its infantry units to ensure surveillance and to enable them to defend the positions that they recently occupied, it was increasingly realised that the Indian troops at high altitudes were desperately short of heavy equipment. Mountain units did not even have the M40A1 106mm recoilless rifles of the units based in the plains. Rather, as noted, their principal direct fire heavy weapon was the M18 57mm recoilless rifle. This was deemed to be inadequate and as a result, India inducted several artillery pieces.

Inducting Artillery

India was also concerned that a Pakistani offensive would need to be countered by additional fire support. As has been noted, the infantry battalions committed to the Siachen operation had their integral support weapons and 81mm mortar platoons were available besides their normal complement of machine guns, platoon-level 51mm mortars and some rocket launchers. Man-portable Grad-P launchers were the principal long-range artillery available to the Siachen troops, supported, if necessary by the ZU-23-2 guns that could be used in the direct fire role. It was increasingly felt that this was inadequate for upcoming operations.

As can be imagined, inducting large artillery pieces would prove a daunting prospect. To this end, a trial was made with a single 105mm IFG Mk.1 from the 108 Medium Regiment. Following its test firing, the weapon was declared operational at the base camp on 10 May 1984. In a display of initiative, one 75/24 pack howitzer was dismantled and carried manually by Indian soldiers over several miles up the rocky and snow-covered glacier to be deployed at an altitude of 16,000 feet. Following the success of the initial 105mm IFG Mk.1, two more guns of the type were deployed to the base camp and by 26 May, several more guns were deployed to Siachen.[66]

Operation Ababeel: The First Battle

Ostensibly, Operation Ababeel was to be Pakistan's own pre-emptive strike at capturing the Siachen Glacier. However, having discovered India's pre-emption of their own pre-emption, the Pakistan Army opened fire at India's positions on 25 April 1984. However, the real Pakistani push came on 23 June 1984 and was intense and determined. Captain Kulkarni described the first sharp exchange on that fateful morning:

> On 22 June 1984, there was shelling on our posts from the Pakistani side. Mostly 120mm mortar fire. It also snowed heavily that day. In the early hours of 23 June, Lance Naik Chanchal Singh was on duty as the LP Sentry. That morning around 4.45hrs, he spotted some movement about one kilometre away. He immediately shouted "*dushman, dushman* [enemy]". But before Chanchal

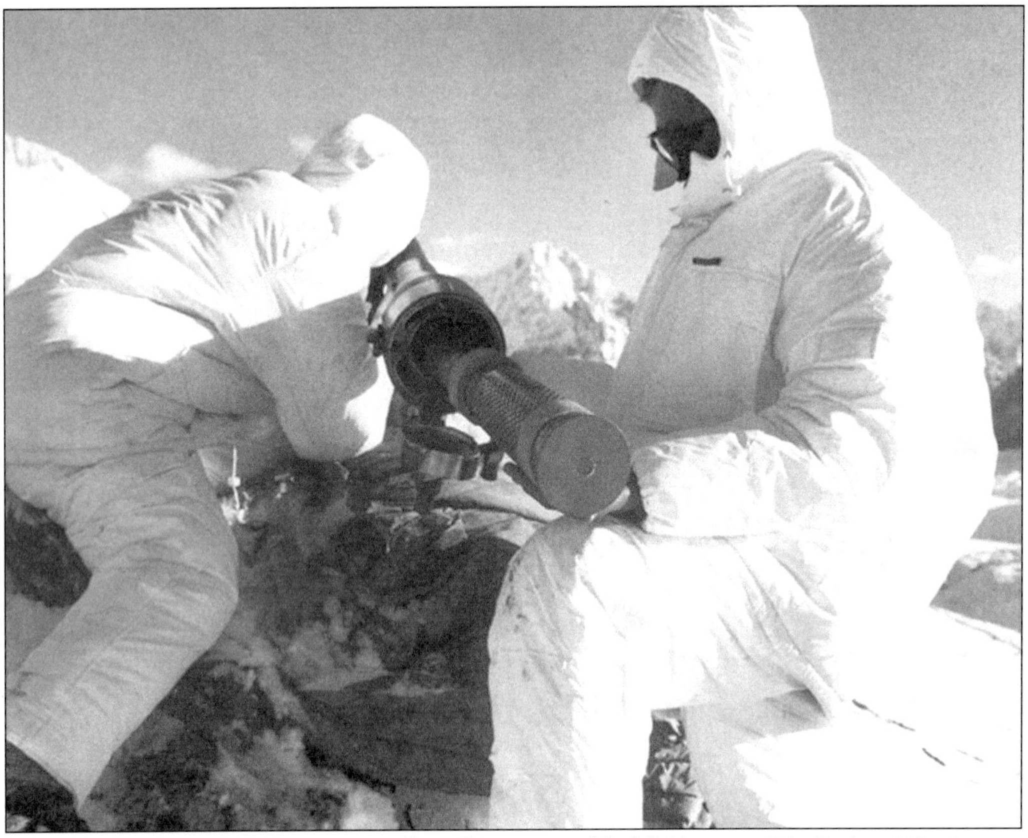

Indian Army troops manning a 106mm recoilless rifle atop one of the hillsides around the Siachen. (Albert Grandolini Collection)

An officer of the Pakistan Army seen communicating by radio with elements of his unit: high mountain peaks and the weather frequently disturbed all means of communication in the Siachen area. (Albert Grandolini Collection)

could run back to the post, he was hit by Pakistani firing. The firing was effective. He died on the spot but managed to alert us. Because of Chanchal and another soldier, Govind Singh on perimeter sentry duty, we were activated immediately. Once they [the Pakistanis] were spotted, it was a matter of getting our act together. When Hav. Sukhbir came rushing and said, "*Saheb, dushman!*" I asked him, are you sure you are not hallucinating? He said "No sir, Chanchal has been hit." I immediately rushed out and then it was all out firing from our side. They stood no chance one we had spotted them…We beat them back and for a full day many bodies lay strewn on the lower slopes.[67]

This initial combat was the first intimation to most of the Indian public and even many in the government, that India had taken control of the Siachen Glacier, had established a military presence at those altitudes and was facing off against Pakistani troops.[68] Indeed, it was the BBC Hindi service that first reported the fighting to the outside world, and outside of Northern Command few even in the army and the broader politic knew of the conflict. An official report of that day's action described the first combat as follows:

> After the first firing incident on 25 April 1984, Pak troops tried to evict us from Bilafond La on 23 June. At approximately 04.45hrs, own listening post located ahead of our own post for early warning, spotted 30-40 enemy troops stealthily moving up the Bilafond glacier. As the leading troops reached 300 to 400 metres ahead of the LP, L/Nk Chanchal Singh and L/Nk Govind Singh of 4 Kumaon opened up with their LMGs on the enemy. The surprise having been lost, Pak troops started firing with all their weapons – HMGs, LMGs and mortars. The fire was very effective. The accurate fire almost made it impossible to carry out any movement between LP and main post.
>
> Unmindful of his personal safety, L/Nk Chanchal Singh, after engaging with the enemy withdrew. Undaunted and aware of the urgency to alert the post, he managed to reach the post and inform the post commander Capt. Kulkarni, and after informing him of the impending attack, succumbed to his injuries. With the enemy closing onto about 500 metres of the post, our own post opened fire with automatic and small arms. Caught in the open, the enemy suffered casualties. Despite losses, Pak troops made two more attempts to capture Bilafond La.
>
> Pak suffered 26 casualties. Pak plans were foiled by the alertness displayed by the LP and the gallant efforts of the post of Bilafond La. This bloody nose to Pak in the first major skirmish in the region had a very salutary effect. Pak troops rolled back from their position at Ali Brangsa to about 7 kilometres SW of Bilafond La. Our troops occupied the area Ring Contour 5369 from where they could effectively dominate the Siachen Glacier.

On the same day, Pak troops made an attempt to move forward and close in our post at Sia La. The attempt was foiled by bringing accurate fire on the enemy. Mortar fire on the enemy camp at Kondus glacier was effective and enemy troops were seen running from their tents. Subsequently the camp was shifted two km southwards along the Kondus.[69]

Living conditions at one of the Pakistani forward operations bases. Note the use of pre-fabricated shelters instead of tents, and blankets laid out to ventilate on top of the shelters. (Albert Grandolini Collection)

This first combat demonstrated that there were severe constraints in conducting offensive operations on the Siachen Glacier. Timely warning of hostile action was essential but not always possible due to the weather. In addition, even the best of troops suffered severe privations and fatigue due to the intense environmental conditions. Yet, the actions of 4 Kumaon against a determined attack stand out for their tenacity in defence. However, as might be suspected owing to the continued secrecy surrounding Operation Meghdoot, even the citations for the gallantry awards for Captain Sanjay Kulkarni and Lance Naik Chanchal Singh were kept somewhat vague.[70]

It was also realised that troops needed to be rotated through spells of duty. Severe mental and physical stress became endemic and Northern Command realised that regular turnover of personnel was essential. This was handicapped by the time needed to acclimatise troops for duty at such extreme altitudes and in such extreme conditions. As such, then, as today, the ability to move and rotate troops to their duty positions on the Siachen Glacier is a time consuming and very involved process that requires many stages of effort and which further requires an extremely intense, and at time precarious, logistics effort.

The troops of 4 Kumaon at Bilafond La and the troops of 19 Kuamon at Gyong La, plus the Ladakh Scouts at Sia La were increasingly exhausted and casualties related to the environment gradually started to mount. It was apparent to Northern Command that troop rotation was needed. Working out an ideal rotation cycle took some effort but General Chibber was to note: 'I had directed that troops deployed on glacial posts be released periodically in about 3-4 months. 1 Vikas (of the SFF) and two companies of Ladakh Scouts were earmarked for the second induction.'[71]

Indian Dispositions After the Initial Clashes

By July 1984, prior to the first turnover of troops – the second induction in General Chibber's words – India's troop deployment on the Siachen Glacier was as follows:

1. At Sia La: One Company Minus [that is, a half-strength company] of the Ladakh Scouts supported by a section of Medium Machine Guns [FN MAG], one section of Heavy Machine Guns [Browning 0.50 cal M2HB], one section of 81mm mortars [two mortars], one detachment of Strela-2M [SA-7] man-portable SAMs and one section of Grad-P, man-portable artillery rockets for direct and indirect fire-support.
2. At Bilafond La: One Company Minus of 4 Kumaon, also supported by a section of MMGs, one section of HMGs, one section of 81mm mortars, one detachment of Strela-2M missiles and one section of Grad-P rockets.
3. At Gyong La: One Company Plus [equivalent to one and one-half companies] of 19 Kumaon, supported by three MMGs, one section of HMGs, one section of 81mm mortars, one detachment of Strela-2M missiles and one section of Grad-P rockets.
4. At Base Camp: 19 Kumaon, minus the equivalent of two companies, deployed at Gyong La and elsewhere supported by one battery of six 105mm IFG Mk.1 field guns.[72]

The decision to replace 19 Kumaon with troops of 1 Vikas at Gyong La proved to be an inspired one. The SFF troops, familiar with the terrain and extremely well-trained, seized the initiative and moved to establish a post at Point 5955, later named Shiv. A supply route through Zingrulma was opened to enable an easing of the supply problem and alleviating the problems faced in the maintenance of the Indian positions at Gyong La. Once Shiv was occupied, the Indian Army brought the entire area under Indian control and observation.[73] Encounters between 1 Vikas and Pakistani troops led to casualties on the latter's part as 1 Vikas took the initiative.

At Sia La, having observed Pakistani activity at their camp ND 6001 on the Kondus Glacier, Indian troops were reinforced by one section of 81mm mortars, two 120mm heavy mortars from a light artillery regiment and some Grad-P rocket launchers. These were moved to the general vicinity of Point 6630 which overlooked the Kondus Glacier. There was an exchange of fire between Indian and Pakistani troops on 30 August 1984 between 11.30hrs and 16.00hrs.[74]

Clashes in August 1984 were reported in both the Gyong La and Sia La areas with Northern Command records saying that a

Pakistani camp was completely destroyed, to the extent of being raised to the ground:

> The enemy suffered heavy casualties of over 20 killed/wounded. A group of personnel, many of them in their pyjamas, were also seen escaping southwards along the Kondus glacier.... On 23 August, at Bilafond La, approximately 30-40 Pakistani personnel were observed moving NE from Ali Brangsa towards our post. Own mortars and Grad P engaged the enemy. The advance elements of 8-10 personnel were killed and more casualties were inflicted when the enemy tried retrieving their bodies.[75]

One of 113 OTO Melara M56 105mm pack howitzers acquired by the Pakistan Army. Even if lacking the robustness necessary for sustained operations, this lightweight weapon proved capable of being disassembled into 12 man-portable components in a matter of minutes: a highly appreciated capability under the conditions of the fighting in the Siachen area. (Pakistan Army)

Pakistan Reinforces and Regroups

In light of these failures, Pakistan's military sought to reinforce their own positions and firepower. Lacking both artillery and even heavy mortars until near the end of August 1984 in any numbers, by 8 September 1984, Northern Command learned through its intelligence sources that instructions had been issued by the HQ of Force Commander Northern Areas, to lift by helicopter, one OTO Melara 105mm pack howitzer to support the ongoing Operation Ababeel. This gun was joined by two more in October.[76]

The effect of this artillery reinforcement was felt when Pakistani troops began using shells fused for both air burst and ground burst against Indian posts at Bilafond La and Gyong La. In addition, Indian intelligence found that through the amalgamation of the commando platoons of several NLI battalions, an ad hoc commando company had been established under the HQ of Pakistan's 80 Infantry Brigade. This unit was to be used to spearhead attacks against Indian positions and, while not up to SSG standards, were very capable in their own right and were a major threat as Operation Ababeel continued in the months to come.[77] To assist their troops deployed at extreme conditions and altitude and taking some advantage of their closer proximity and better access, Pakistan began acquiring alpine huts, three of which arrived in Skardu by September 1984.

Indian Army soldier on a counterinsurgency operation near the Line of Control. (Albert Grandolini Collection)

India's Administrative and Infrastructure Build Up

After four months, in the aftermath of Operations Meghdoot and despite Operation Ababeel still being underway, the military and geographic situation had stabilised but India sought to hold the initiative on the Saltoro Ridge. These positions, it was becoming ever more apparent, would need to be held permanently and this inevitably meant that India was going to need a major effort to provide adequate support and logistics to its troops on the Siachen Glacier.

As a first step, the track from Sasoma to the Siachen base camp was improved, at first to enable the easy movement of a 3-ton truck. This path would later be turned into a smooth, all-weather road capable of taking much heavier traffic. One of the IAF's newly arrived AN-32 transport aircraft was brought into theatre to move additional supplies to the Indian troops with much more care than was hitherto the norm, being paid to troop comfort, mental, physical and material well-being:

> Attention was also paid for improving the material comfort of the troops. Fibre glass shelters, procured off the shelf (ex-trade

is the Army term) were constructed by Army engineers at the glacial posts. Recreation facilities, including VCRs and TV sets were also installed for improving the morale of the troops and keeping them engaged. Research and development activity to improve living conditions and survival were also undertaken. The Snow and Avalanche Study Establishment (SASE), to assist in the collection of data to study the environmental conditions in the region was also established.[78]

Thus, as 1984 drew to an end, India's military engagement in the Siachen theatre of operations was thus in progress. It remains to date, India's longest military engagement.

5
THE WIDENING CONFLICT

By 1985, the dictatorship of General Zia-ul-Haq in Pakistan was being challenged by a resurgent opposition led by Benazir Bhutto, the daughter of former Prime Minister Zulfikar Ali Bhutto who had been hanged by General Zia in 1979. She taunted the Pakistani government and targeted General Zia for losing Siachen to India. Once politics entered the equation, and ever wary of its own dubious legitimacy and the undemocratic nature of his own government, General Zia felt compelled to make efforts to retake the Siachen Glacier. This set the tone for a series of heavy military engagements in 1985 and the years thereafter, to the great cost of both armies.

Nitin Gokhale, an Indian military expert of note, quoted Peter R. Levoy, who – in his book *Asymetric Warfare in South Asia: The Causes and Consequences of the Kargil Conflict* – wrote:

> The Pakistani army sees India's 1984 occupation of Siachen as a major scar, outweighed only by Dhaka's fall in 1971. The event underscored the dilution of the Shimla Agreement and became a domestic issue as political parties, led by Benazir Bhutto's People's Party, blamed an incompetent military government under Zia ul-Haq for failing to defend Pakistani-held territory – while Zia downplayed the significance of the loss.[1]

Political Overtones: Widening Conflict and Increasing Costs

Benazir Bhutto did have a legitimate argument as the Pakistan Army's X Corps had a strong indication that India would try to occupy the passes on the Saltoro Ridge. As seen previously, X Corps had started its preparations to pre-empt any such Indian move and was in some ways at an even more advanced stage of planning than India. However, thanks to some unconventional Indian thinking and Brigadier Channa's decision to move on 13 April 1984, Pakistan's efforts were themselves pre-empted and this led to India being able to occupy higher ground and entrench itself into sound defensible positions, simultaneously bringing up more supplies and artillery.

As a result of it being caught by surprise at India's actions, as well as being repeatedly stung by the criticisms from its domestic opposition, Pakistan's army embarked upon a series of efforts to dislodge India from the ridges and to occupy these features. While these efforts, even had they succeeded, would have given the Pakistan Army no tactical advantage, it compelled India to commit additional resources in manpower and material to secure and garrison all possible heights when merely holding the passes would have sufficed for India's strategic and tactical military purposes. In this regard, politics trumped sound strategy.[2] This was to prove costly for both sides in terms of casualties but more so for Pakistan as it was attacking uphill to deal with Indian positions on heights and on the ridge lines. This inevitably gave a significant advantage to the defending forces which they used to great effect in the battles that were to come in the 1980s. India was to exploit this advantage to telling effect in a series of engagements.

Pakistan's army, being under pressure to respond to India's Operation Meghdoot began to muster additional forces and their assorted material for an offensive operation. India's Northern Command intelligence estimated that a Task Force HQ had been carved out of 62 Infantry Brigade and established at Khapalu to coordinate operations against Indian positions on the Siachen and Saltoro. In addition, elements from 323 Infantry Brigade, located at Gilgit, were moved forward with a view to their conducting kinetic operations on the Siachen Glacier. The Northern Command appreciation further noted:

> The following units were officially part of the Siachen deployment from the Pakistani side by November – December 1984: 21 POK Battalion, 1 Northern Light Infantry (NLI) Battalion supported by one company of 9 NLI and one company (Shaheen) of 1 SSG Battalion. An independent mountain battery from the 452 (I) Artillery Regiment equipped with 105mm guns, one battery of 88 (I) Medium Battery equipped with 120mm mortars and an *ad hoc* company raised under the 80 Infantry Brigade.[3]

Indian Dispositions and Rotation of Troops

In November 1984, just in time for the winter and coming conflicts of 1985, Northern Command was starting the third turnover of Indian troops on the Siachen Glacier. It was soon realised that given Pakistan's continued interest in dislodging Indian troops from their positions, Northern Command would have to bring into theatre ever-increasing numbers of troops as well as the attendant logistics and material plus the necessary supporting artillery and other support weapons, all to be supported by an ever-increasing air bridge using a combination of fixed wing transport aircraft and various helicopters.

Northern Command records of the situation at the end of 1984, as accessed by Nitin Gokhale in perhaps the definitive work on India's Siachen operations, noted:

> With the decision to occupy the Siachen region permanently throughout the year, the third induction of troops was planned. Despite extreme weather conditions with temperatures falling below minus 30 degrees Celsius, exchange of fire was almost a daily routine. Logistics problems were further exaggerated because of the increased requirements of kerosene at all posts and replenishment of ammunition. The Pakistani build up meanwhile continued unabated especially opposite Sia La and Gyong La.[4]

Further troop inductions were also made in theatre with the various battalions now being more properly attached to existing brigades. By November 1984, 2 Vikas was located at Tangste under 114 Infantry Brigade which was dual tasked with looking after the frontier with China in Eastern Ladakh (of considerably more importance today). This unit was brought in to relieve 1 Vikas which had served with distinction and now returned to its original location at Kiari, under the control of 70 Infantry Brigade.

From 2 Vikas, one company was deployed to Bilafond La and two more companies of 2 Vikas were sent to take up positions at Gyong La. The Ladakh Scouts continued to hold their positions, and be responsible for Sia La. These units held their positions until April 1985 when they were replaced by fresh troops, properly acclimatised and equipped.[5]

Some troops, such as the ski troopers from HAWS and assorted volunteers were withdrawn as it was becoming difficult to sustain them in the harsh winters and because the mission had now shifted to a long-term deployment as opposed to a short-term, though high-risk operation. These logistical difficulties were to prove a near-continuous challenge with helicopter sorties being severely limited because of very high winds as well as extremely limited visibility. With the relatively poor avionics aboard the Cheetahs, operating at extreme altitude, this could and did pose a major hazard to the aircraft. In very severe conditions, besides the normal concerns of supply, casualty evacuation and the relief of troops was an additional problem that had to be addressed. As Northern Command was to record:

> During the extreme cold conditions coupled with snow blizzards, we had approximately 10 clear days in a month for flying. The low temperatures reduced efficiency of the troops and weapons to a large extent. Added to this, the wind chill factor made living conditions almost unbearable. This resulted in a number of casualties due to extreme cold and chill, further adding to logistics problems of evacuation and relief.[6]

With the Pakistani build up well in progress, India initially anticipated a Pakistani offensive in the summer of 1985. However, on a routine air operations helicopter sortie to Sia La on 21 February, the Indian crew spotted three Pakistani positions close to a peak known as Saddle that had hitherto remained unoccupied. This sparked immediate concern in Indian circles and prompted a further investigation, once again by helicopter to ascertain whether this was the portent for another offensive or something that was rather more benign.[7]

The redoubtable Brigadier Vijay Channa, whose brilliance had secured the Siachen Glacier and the Saltoro passes for India, had now been replaced by Brigadier Jal Master, having completed his tenure with distinction. Brigadier Master now commanded the new 102 Infantry Brigade. This was converted from the old 26 Sector and was now to become the designation of the brigade assigned to the Siachen Glacier ever since, with various battalions rotating through the brigade, thus blooding the Indian Army in extreme high altitude conditions and providing a cadre of operational and administrative experience and continuity. This Pakistani deployment was its first test.[8]

Brigadier Master, having been apprised of the apparent intrusion, decided to undertake an aerial reconnaissance of the area in person. Once he noticed the Pakistani dispositions, he immediately ordered a patrol of near platoon strength from the Ladakh Scouts – one officer, one JCO and 20 other ranks – to move towards and occupy Saddle NL 375003, which was located near enough to the Pakistani encampments in the vicinity. Now that Indian troops were present and in adequate, though not generous, numbers, the Indians waited for the inevitable Pakistani attack. This attack finally came at around 12.00hrs on 22 February 1985.[9]

Pakistani forces moved against the Indian position at Saddle but were held by the small force of Ladakh Scouts under the command of Major M.S. Dahiya. For five hours the Pakistanis tried to break through at Saddle but after these attacks failed, they attempted to interdict the track between Saddle and Sia La at night. Thanks to alert troops, these attacks were thwarted and India believes that it killed at least five Pakistani soldiers, three of which were confirmed through intercepts. The action of 22 February was short and sharp but was not to be the last.[10]

The Indian positions on Saddle were not fully entrenched and desperately short of supplies and after the intense action, of the 22 February, was in need of resupply. However, the weather took a dangerous turn for the worse and at dawn on the 23 February, it was sufficiently bad that only five Cheetah helicopter sorties could be launched to resupply the Ladakh Scout patrol on Saddle with ammunition and rations. The Pakistanis launched another attack on the 23-24 February, this time with fire support from mortars and artillery, but this was beaten back despite its intensity.[11]

The Year After Meghdoot

As the first anniversary of India's audacious Operation Meghdoot came around, there was a serious evaluation of the situation as it pertained to Indian deployment on the Siachen Glacier and the Saltoro Ridge. It was abundantly clear that Pakistan would not desist from its efforts to wrest control of the glacier and the passes from India. This sparked a review of the force levels needed to preserve India's positions. This would inevitably entail additional troops and the attendant supplies, support equipment and logistical infrastructure to sustain them for a prolonged, high altitude deployment.

In its review in the summer of 1985, Northern Command was clear in its view that the Pakistani attacks of February 1985 were a portent of things to come and noted:

> By the third week of April 1985, there had been a perceptible hardening in Pakistan's attitude and stance as regards operations on the Siachen Glacier. This was evident from the intransigent attitude adopted by Pakistan during various flag meetings culminating in their abortive attempt to evict us from Sia La in February 1985.[12]

Following these attacks in February 1985, India realised that despite its occupation of the peaks, it could not effectively observe any movement of Pakistani troops on the Gyong Glacier. To remedy this situation, India decided to take a feature that it designated, in the absence of any proper name, NL 60654. The task of capturing this feature was given to the Ladakh Scouts under the command of a JCO, Naib Subedar Rinchen, who successfully seized the feature on 17 June 1985 without the Pakistan Army being aware of this Indian activity. Northern Command was to note:

> For the next three days the enemy was unaware of our presence in this area which gave us the opportunity to consolidate and expand 'Rinchen' (that is how posts came to be names, mostly after soldiers who ventured into the unknown and established Indian presence. So you have several posts – Ajay, Bhim-Sonam, Amar,

to cite just a few – named after daring warriors) into a formidable locality. After establishment of 'Rinchen' and 'Das' (another post named after a soldier), we were able to completely dominate the enemy from Lake Camp to OP II. This strangulation move in conjunction with establishment of 'Das' completely surprised and harassed the enemy. Because of its crucially dominating location, the outpost at 'Rinchen' has inflicted a large number of casualties on the enemy.[13]

An Alouette III of the Pakistan Army Aviation (serial number 1454) about to land at a forward operating base in the Siachen area. (Albert Grandolini Collection)

These small battles began to make India realise that Pakistan had no intention of leaving India in peaceful possession of this territory. Politics, pride and nationalism all came into play and both sides became embroiled in an intense confrontation that flared up into active combat relatively infrequently but were to present an ever-present danger and fears of escalation always loomed large over the heads of decision makers.

Lessons of 1985

Thus, by the summer of 1985, Northern Command had to face the fact that it was facing a prolonged deployment. Unsurprisingly, it duly informed the Army HQ in Delhi that it required a larger deployment of troops to prevent Pakistan from taking any of the passes: the army had to establish permanent presence there. The GHQ in New Delhi originally envisaged a battalion-level deployment – about 1,000 troops in total. This rapidly grew to a brigade-level deployment – 3,000 men plus supporting artillery and logistics. Another increase followed in the aftermath of the Kargil War of 1999, by when it reached a division-level deployment – some 15,500 personnel. Unsurprisingly, since 1985, the 102 Infantry Brigade has been designated the 'Siachen Brigade'.[14]

Pakistan held a significant logistical advantage over India as the road to Gyong La was close enough to allow for a turnaround time of only four days as opposed to 10 in India's case. This is even more pronounced at Sia La where Pakistan can turn around troops in a mere six days while India takes around 15 days. This presented India with a significant logistical challenge compounded by the need to acclimatise, support and maintain troops in extreme conditions, not to mention occasional combat.

It has been said that a single platoon of 30 requires a company of 100 to maintain the platoon in sufficient shape to fight any sort of major battle with an adversary that enjoyed freedom to concentrate its forces at points of its choosing. This inevitably meant that India would have to commit ever more resources to its Siachen operations, both manpower and material.

General Chibber, ever aware of these major issues, recommended that India enhance its deployment of forces, up to and including the strengthening of air defences. Additional support from the engineers, the signals and ordnance and service branches were ever more necessary. Being very aware of what he was asking, in a note to Army HQ, General Chibber wrote:

> Earlier, basically because of problems of logistics and air maintenance, we had taken a decision to adopt 'summer' and 'winter' postures in the area of Operation Meghdoot. The Pakistani attempt to dislodge us from the weakened Sia La position in winter, which had to rapidly reinforce, gave us anxious moments between 21 February and 1 March. With a much shorter turnaround of Pakistani troops from their road head, we could not take the risk of thinning out during winter. There could be no summer or winter postures, barring pulling back of some posts established in summer months on the heights which were untenable in winter.[15]

General Chibber recommended a major increase in India's force levels in the area and further suggested enhancing supporting elements, to sustain a long duration deployment as follows:

- Artillery: One Air Defence Battery, one Grad P artillery regiment, one light regiment of 120mm mortars, one field regiment of 105mm field guns and one six gun battery from a medium regiment – either 130mm M-46 or, later 155mm Bofors FH-77-B02
- Engineers: One Field Company
- Signals: One Line Section, half a radio section and two mobile signals detachments
- Infantry: Two additional Infantry Battalions
- Air Support: Six Cheetah helicopters, two Mi-8 helicopters with four AN-32 transport aircraft to transport bulk items for onward movement by helicopter
- Army Service Corps: One Composite Platoon; and two motor transport platoons with 3 ton trucks
- Army Medical Corps: One Advance Dressing Station and one technical support platoon

- Electrical and Mechanical Engineers: One Advance Workshop Detachment.[16]

Reinforcements at this level stretched the resources of 3 Infantry Division to its limits with all uncommitted reserves being exhausted by the summer of 1985. This required additional formations and support elements to be drafted into theatre from other locations in India. The scope of Operation Meghdoot now extended to the physical domination of the Saltoro watershed, stretching from Sia La in the north to NJ 9842 to the south, posing a very heavy burden.[17]

This entire effort was increasingly reliant on air support and the helicopters of the Indian Air Force, prior to the formation of the Army Aviation Corps, bore the full brunt of both aerial surveillance and transport to the highest points of Indian control. The IAF operated Air Observation Post squadrons – Air OP squadrons – which carried out observation tasks for Indian artillery. These units were equipped with a mix of Cheetah and Chetak helicopters – license-built versions of the Alouette II and Alouette III respectively. The Cheetah, in particular, was to prove of immense value owing to its incredible ability to operate at high altitudes, albeit with very limited payloads. General Chibber's requirement of six Cheetahs and two Mi-8 helicopters was to prove easy to meet in 1985 but as the years, and decades passed, it became clear that a greater number of helicopters of both light and medium types needed to be deployed in theatre.

Military Operations from 1987 to 1999

In April 1987, Pakistan began a sustained effort to regain the initiative on the Siachen Glacier. This effort was spearheaded by the troops of its excellent SSG. In an astonishing feat of mountaineering, a platoon of the SSG was able to occupy the southern shoulder (also called the 'left shoulder') of the Bilafond La Pass which dominated the whole Bilafond La area. At an elevation of 21,184 feet, Pakistan established the Quaid Post without the Indian forces in the area, or in position at the Amar and Sonam posts becoming aware of their movement, much less success.[18]

The first the Indian Army learned of this Pakistani post was when on 18 April 1987, a Pakistani machine gun team – using MG3 machine guns – opened fire on India's Sonam post, some 1,500 metres below, and killed two Indian soldiers of the 5 Bihar Regiment. Helicopters ferrying supplies to Sonam and Amar were now increasingly coming under heavy and accurate machine gun fire, thus placing India's Amar and Sonam posts in some danger and making their continued occupation increasingly untenable and short of abandoning them, some solution to the Quaid Post problem had to be found. India decided to eliminate the post.

As April is still the heart of winter on the Siachen Glacier, and considering that the left shoulder of the Bilafond La Pass is at an 85 degree incline for a distance of over 500 metres, any attacking force would be instantly detected and neutralised by the Pakistani garrison without difficulty, especially by the well-entrenched SSG supported by adequate crew-served weapons. Another solution had to be found and one which had a reasonable chance of achieving the objective.

One suggestion was the use of helicopter gunships. In 1987, the IAF operated a number of AS.11-equipped Chetak helicopters in a single helicopter unit and another with Mi-25 helicopters in a more diverse close air support role with rockets, gun-pods and bombs besides ATGMs. In addition, the Mi-8 helicopters could also be armed with rocket pods and machine guns. However, in the rarefied atmosphere of the Siachen Glacier and against a target situated on a narrow peak, such an operation would be unlikely to succeed. In fact, the Mi-25 and Chetak were singularly unsuitable to operations at extreme altitudes.[19]

Machine gunners of the Pakistan Army, with MG3 machine gun, in position in the Siachen area. (Pakistan Army)

The Indian plan to take Quaid Post was formulated by Brigadier C.S. Nugyal, second in command of 102 Infantry Brigade. His plan was borne out of necessity and involved a frontal assault on the Pakistani post. Their effort required a careful reconnaissance of the position and to this end, a ten-person team, led by Second Lieutenant Rajiv Pandey of 8 JAK LI was given the task. However, even assembling this team and getting it in position proved to be very difficult owing to the limitations of air transport. It took some 35 Cheetah helicopter sorties to transport the team and some three weeks to build up resources.[20]

On 29 May 1987, Pandey led nine men up a 90 degree climb on ice walls to assault Quaid Post. This was an effort doomed to disaster. The troops survived for two days without food or water as they affixed ropes to scale the near-vertical ice wall but as they neared the Pakistani positions, the SSG team detected the Indian assault and opened fire, killing Pandey, his second in command and six other Indian soldiers – eight of the 10 Indian attackers thus being killed in this initial assault. This led to a revision of tactics with the Indian battalion intent on revenge.[21]

It was appreciated that the assault would be difficult and could involve heavy fighting and require the use of artillery. Northern Command kept Army HQ informed of developments as escalation was an ever-present risk. There was the additional problem of putting the assault team together as there was a surplus of volunteers. Brigadier Rajiv Williams was to note:

> When volunteers were asked to raise this force, there was not a single person who remained silent; everyone wanted to participate and take revenge. The objective had to be captured, and the

Pakistanis had to be put in their place. Since the men were distributed at various posts in groups of 10 to 15, with a mix of personnel from supporting services, it was not possible to get personnel from just one company… After a quick, deliberate selection process, keeping the factor of immediate availability, a force of 50 men was selected with Major Virender Singh as Task Force Commander and Captain Anil Sharma as his 2IC (Second in Command).'[22]

Operation Quiadat began with an intense artillery preparation provided by OTO Melara M56 pack howitzers of the Pakistan Army. (Pakistan Army)

At the end of May, the Task Force moved to the Indian administrative base some one kilometre away from the left shoulder at Bilafond La. For the force – two officers, three JCOs and 57 other ranks (62 in totals) – that was to make the assault, no fewer than 200 Cheetah helicopter sorties were needed. Initial probes to find the ropes left by 2nd Lt. Pandey proved abortive and while a second platoon led by Subedar Sansar Singh succeeded in finding the ropes, the attack did not go through owing to a communications gap between the Task Force and the respective platoon. This meant that India required a third assault to try to evict the Pakistanis from Quaid.[23]

This third assault was led by Naib Subedar Bana Singh who led a team of riflemen – Chunni Lal, Laxman Das, Om Raj and Kashmir Chand – at 12.11hrs on 26 June 1987 for the final assault on Quaid Post. After an arduous climb, Bana Singh and his team reached the Pakistani post in heavy snowfall and extremely bad weather and there they confronted the single Pakistani bunker manned by Naib Subedar Atta Mohammed of the Shaheen Company of the SSG and a small Pakistani force. Heavy, close-quarters fighting took place leading to India's capture of the post and the death of six Pakistani soldiers. In recognition of his enormous bravery and effort, Quaid Post was renamed Bana Top.[24]

Operations Quiadat and VajraShakti

In September 1987, the SSG, which became Pakistan's strike force in Siachen, prepared another strike against Bilafond La. This might have been the brainchild of Brigadier, later General and then President, Pervez Musharraf. Codenamed Operation Quiadat, the Pakistani assault was aimed at capturing two Indian posts, Ashok and U-Cut. Ashok was lightly held by only eight Indian soldiers led by Naib Subedar Lekh Raj. This post was then subject to an intense artillery barrage, as were all the Indian posts in the Bilafond La. This was the beginning of some of the heaviest fighting in the Siachen conflict.

On 23 September 1987, Pakistan began its assault on Ashok. The assault was led by 1 and 3 Battalions of the SSG and supported by 2 NLI. Brigadier Rajiv Williams, then a major at Sonam Post, described the battle as follows, speaking as many Indian soldiers do, with admiration of the Pakistani SSG and its bravery:

> At precisely 5.55hrs, the brave, young and courageous men of Pakistan's elite SSG obeyed orders of their commander and at the break of dawn were seen trudging along the narrow ridge leading to Ashok. The deployability along the ridge was no more than two men abreast, and therefore we could observe scores of rows following one behind the other. The attack had commenced… Ashok Post was held by only a weak section of 8 men of 8 JAK LI and later strengthened by reinforcements from 3/4 Gorkha Rifles…
>
> Having waited for the attack till close to 3.00hrs, we had barely slept on the night of 22-23 September, when I received a radio communication from the JCO positioned at Ashok, saying that the Pakistanis were coming on to the post in large numbers. Initially, I thought the report was not correct, because who in their right mind would venture an uphill assault in the early hours of the morning. However, the report was correct and the enemy was climbing that steep ridgeline and could be observed distinctly – a delightful opportunity for our troops. The Pakistanis were appropriately welcomed by Lekh Raj along with seven other men. The [Pakistani] numbers swelled, but Lekh Raj kept assuring us that nothing would happen to the post as long as he was alive… It was not more than 15 minutes after he spoke with me over the radio set when a TOW missile fired from the enemy fire base hit the bunker directly and killed the JCO instantaneously along with two other men.[25]

Intense fighting took place over the next few days with India ploughing reinforcements into the fray and to Ashok post. An Indian counterstroke, codenamed Operation VajraShakti was prepared and made extensive use of artillery. Suresh Nair, an officer then with 314 Field Regiment described his role:

> The 314 Field Regiment was a very young unit, having been raised only in 1984. Immediately on raising we were sent to the glacier and believe me we could not have got a better training ground.

An Indian soldier with a 7.62mm 1B Light Machine Gun (a slightly modernised Bren gun) in position on the Siachen Glacier. (Indian Army)

The bottom view of a Lama helicopter of the Pakistan Army Aviation Corps, deploying a soldier to a forward position with a help of the winch. It was in similar fashion that the Pakistanis deployed two of their troops atop the peak of the Churmik Glacier in March 1989. (Pakistan Army)

On 23 September when the attack began, early morning and as the section located on the Ashok post kept fighting gallantly, we in the artillery started firing our medium, light and field guns on the enemy positions. By 11.30hrs the enemy had to withdraw and take cover behind the Tola hill and the HMG ridge. The arty [artillery] duel carried on with deadly salvos of air burst and ground burst ammunition. Mainly air burst ammunition was used with great effect. The adversary once again started shelling Ashok and U-Cut on the night of 24 September and seen approaching Ashok in a platoon strength with some civilian porters. The platoon was followed by a whole battalion in four columns. Our artillery fire was readjusted on these advancing columns and they were stalled.

During this battle we employed three 130mm guns, three 105mm LFGs and three 120mm mortars. Artillery in the three nights fired over 3,000 rounds of ammunition, which must be a record from the small number of guns. One 130mm gun burst on the last night due to the intensity of firing, as also the large number of rounds fired. An intercepted radio communication revealed a Pakistani company commander telling his superiors that no movement was possible due to the very heavy and accurate artillery shelling.[26]

Finally, on the 25 September 1987, after three days and nights of heavy fighting, the Pakistanis withdrew. Casualties, as is always the case, were heavily disputed. India claimed that it had killed or wounded over 300 Pakistanis while admitting to the loss of 20 men. Pakistan disputed these claims but there is little doubt that Pakistan's attack ended in abject failure, as did a more minor probe in October 1987.[27] These costly operations had a salutary effect on the course of operations on the Siachen Glacier and heavy fighting, and large-scale operations were significantly reduced with both sides recognising the difficulty of sustaining operations at that altitude.

Operation Ibex

In March 1989, Pakistan once again tried to neutralise Indian positions at Bilafond La. This time, in a stunning operation, two Pakistani soldiers, strapped to the landing gear of a helicopter by rope, were successfully inserted into a peak at the Chumik Glacier, at an altitude of 19,000 feet. Indian attempts to dislodge the Pakistanis from their position by direct assault were beaten off by these two soldiers who held out for 36 hours before reinforcements arrived to bolster their presence. However, even this effort did not succeed in securing any advantage for Pakistan as, in May 1989, Indian troops, led by Brigadier R.K. Nanavatty began a systematic targeting of Pakistan's logistics links and bases to the Chumik Glacier and heavy artillery bombardment managed to destroy Pakistan's Kauser logistics node. The Pakistani troops at Chumik were then withdrawn.[28]

After 1989, the battlefield was relatively quiet, with minor skirmishes erupting. Between 28 July and 3 August 1992, there was a Pakistani attack against India's Bahadur post. The attack was repulsed and in the ensuing combat, on 2 August 1992 Indian Igla-1M man-portable SAMs were fired at Pakistani helicopters, one of which, – an Alouette II – carrying the Force Commander Northern Areas, Brigadier Masood Navid Anwari, was shot down causing the Pakistani offensive to be halted and operations were subsequently discontinued.[29]

Another encounter took place in 1995. On the night of 16-17 May 1995, another Pakistani attack, this time made against the Indian post at Tyakshi by 200 NLI soldiers was supported by the Pakistani Rangers. The Indian troops stationed at the post lured them into a killing zone with no fewer than six machine guns and two mortars being targeted on the Pakistanis, causing the attack to disintegrate with heavy loss of life, with the bodies of the dead Pakistani soldiers being recovered subsequently under a flag of truce as was the norm.[30]

The 1990s would see periodic clashes but nobody predicted that in 1999, India and Pakistan would go to war, shortly after conducting nuclear tests in 1998, over a region of Kashmir which posed a major concern for India regarding its ability to sustain operations in Siachen. This led to the 1999 Kargil War which would alter the security dynamic in the region.

6 KARGIL WAR, 1999

The Kargil War was a watershed in India-Pakistan relations. The conflict was the subcontinent's first media war, with Indian journalists from the dynamic and diverse print media as well as a new generation of young and competent television correspondents flocking to the Kargil region to give first-hand accounts. This helped to cement support for the war among the Indian public, which was treated to the spectacle of coffins draped in the Indian tricolour coming back from the battlefield. Correspondents to the Kargil theatre of operations also brought home to the Indian public the effort of the Indian Army and the conditions under which operations were conducted. It was also the first armed conflict between the two countries in the aftermath of their 1998 nuclear weapon tests.

Siachen Connection

In 1999, very indirectly, the Siachen conflict played a part in the bloody war between India and Pakistan in the Kargil region of Ladakh. This war was intense, widely-covered in the media and provokes strong feelings. From an Indian perspective, the Kargil Conflict brought out serious shortcomings in India's national security apparatus, caused much internal debate and ultimately led to an expert panel review and the failures which allowed the Pakistani incursion to occur. The report produced by the Kargil Review Committee, was released and published in a redacted form and forms an important body of work on the subject of the war, being unsparing in criticism, recommending major changes to the then-existing system as well as crediting the ability of even the flawed Indian system to respond effectively to a threat.

As in earlier times, the primary means of resupplying Pakistani troops during the infiltration attempts of 1999 remained Alouette III helicopters of the Pakistan Army Aviation Corps. Their crews went well beyond what might be expected of them to keep the troops well-stocked with ammunition, food and other necessities. This Alouette was photographed while collecting a load from one of the forward operating bases at lower altitudes. (Albert Grandolini Collection)

From a Pakistani perspective, it is rather unfortunate that even to date there is a degree of reticence to acknowledge the extent of Pakistan's role in the conflict, the units of its armed forces involved, as well as the extent of their losses. It was only after a gap of 13 years that the names of some of the soldiers of the NLI were acknowledged to have fallen in combat during the Kargil Conflict. Even to date, despite a few books on the subject, Pakistan has not taken full ownership of its responsibility for the conflict.

An Alouette II of the Pakistan Army, after landing to resupply a forward observation post in the late 1990s. (Albert Grandolini Collection)

In 1998, India and Pakistan tested nuclear weapons. This was followed by attempts to lower tensions through the so-called Lahore Declaration. However, shortly thereafter the Kargil War between the Republic of India and the Islamic Republic of Pakistan might be deemed to have started on 3 May 1999 and ended on 26 July 1999, making it a relatively long conflict by the standards of the Indian subcontinent.

What began with an infiltration by the troops of the Northern Light Infantry Brigade of the Pakistan Army, supported by separatist 'Mujahidden' combatants into Indian controlled territory, saw the first use of air power by India since the 1971 India-Pakistan War and marked a turning point in relations between the two nations, increasing India's distrust of Pakistan and placing little faith in that country's civilian leadership, which was shortly thereafter toppled.

It is as yet somewhat unclear as to why Pakistan conceived its war plans for Kargil. This is particularly so given that the summit in February 1999 demonstrated a good deal of hope that the tensions between the two countries could be reduced. It might be speculated that Pakistan's army, which has demonstrated a long institutional memory, had sought to initiate Operation Badr to in some way carry out a degree of 'revenge' for India's 1984 Operation Meghdoot.

This is still speculative and it is equally possible that the operation had more to do with the inner machinations of the Pakistani deep state and an attempt to undermine both a civilian government and any possible lowering of tensions with India with an eye on preserving its own interests and influence over the Pakistani government. Any success would accrue to the credit of the military and deep state while failure could be fobbed off as being a result of weak civilian leadership with the attendant political consequences.

All three of India's principal agencies – Research and Analysis Wing (RAW), Intelligence Bureau (IB) and Military Intelligence (MI) – failed to anticipate and to predict Pakistan's actions in Kargil and must therefore share the responsibility for India's initial failures.

The Pakistani incursions were based upon exploitation of the gaps that existed in the defences in the sector both on the Indian and Pakistan side of the LoC due to the geography, with the terrain being extremely rugged. Very few tracks lead from the main roads towards the LoC making transport and reinforcement difficult. The climate also favoured the timing of the operation as during winter the Kargil area receives very heavy snowfall making movement almost impossible and the only mountain pass connecting the Kargil area to the Kashmir Valley, Zoji La, did not usually open until the end of May or beginning of June. This made the movement of Indian reinforcements by road convoys from Srinagar impossible.

Cutting off Siachen: Pakistan's Gameplan

General V.P. Malik, then the Indian Chief of Army Staff, summarised the military objectives as follows:

- Occupy approximately 700 square kilometres area on the Indian side of the LoC in Kargil-Turtuk Sector.
- Interdict Srinagar-Kargil-Leh Road.
- Capture Turtuk and cut off Southern and Central parts of Siachin Glacier Sector, and
- Intensify militants' activities in J&K, which had received a setback after the State Assembly and National Parliament elections in 1997-98.[1]

Brigadier Gurneet Kanwal, who has written extensively on the Kargil War, suggests related but slightly different objectives as follows:

- Phase 1 – Infiltrate militants into the area to subvert locals and initiate insurgency.
- Phase 2 – Launch operations to occupy critical areas around Turtok and the adjacent areas.
- Phase 3 – Launch heliborne/airborne operations in the rear areas of Turtok sector to facilitate operations of ground forces.

The heaviest helicopter deployed by the Pakistan Army in support of its troops in the crisis zone was the French-made Aérospatiale SA.330 Puma. The type proved capable of hauling troops, armament and supplies – and evacuating casualties – to altitudes over 6,000 metres. (Albert Grandolini Collection)

- Phase 4 – Declare Turtok and its adjacent areas as part of the Northern Areas.

Kanwal further opined that the Indian Army Headquarters had the view that Pakistan's military aims were:

- Cut off the strategic National Highway 1A (Srinagar-Leh highway).
- Alter the status of the LoC.
- Give impetus to insurgency in Kashmir Valley and elsewhere in J&K.[2]

Both Brigadier Kanwal and General Singh strongly believed that cutting off the supply lines to support India's Siachen Brigade entered into the Pakistan Army's calculations when Operation Badr was conceived. Any interdiction or disruption of those supply lines could have rendered the Siachen Brigade's positions unsustainable and could have also enabled a Pakistani move to dislodge Indian troops from the positions they currently occupied through a combination of military pressure and supply constraints. It was probably because of this threat that India responded as strongly as it did to dislodge the Pakistani intruders.

From a tactical and operational standpoint, Pakistan conceived a masterpiece: it kept the plan for the infiltration into Kargil – codenamed the Operation Badr – top secret and maintained the element of surprise, totally deceiving multiple Indian intelligence services. The idea for Operation Badr envisaged that no additional units of the Pakistan Army would be inducted into the Force Command Northern Area: this ensured that India's attention would not be piqued by any movement of troops – not even at battalion level. Artillery units inducted in July to September 1998, during a period of heavy exchanges of artillery fire along the LoC, were not pulled back and as such attracted any fresh attention. Pakistan's army undertook no movement of reserve formations or their support elements, and created no new administrative bases. All operations were catered for using existing facilities and made use of existing defensive infrastructure. Logistics were handled along the ridgelines and nullahs, away from Indian units already in position. Moreover, it was only after the Kargil operation had been executed and after the Indian response had started that fresh troops were inducted on the Pakistani side.

Pakistan's Kargil plan was put into action at the end of April 1999. Small sub-groups of platoon size were used to conduct multiple intrusions along the ridgelines and occupy heights dominating Indian positions. After it was finalised, the plan was put into action towards the end of April.

The forces earmarked for the intrusion and used therein were a mixture of highly professional soldiers and Islamist combatants. Units involved included the 3rd, 4th, 5th, 6th and 12th battalions of the Pakistan Army's Northern Light Infantry. The NLI is an old and capable formation with a pedigree going back to the 1950s. Headquarters of 62 Brigade of the Pakistan Army was made responsible administratively for all operations in the Kargil Sector and was responsible for organising, supporting and where possible assisting the infiltration. Supplementing these were operatives from the elite Special Services Group and various Pakistan-based Islamist militants. Moreover, some former Pakistani officers in retrospect criticised the operation as poorly conceived with ridges being occupied by Pakistani troops with no actual ability to sustain operations if cut off.

Defending Pakistani Positions

Following the end of heavy snowfalls, NLI soldiers crossed the LoC in large numbers in the Mushko Valley, Dras, Kaksar and Batalik sub-sectors and established positions on the top of high mountain ridgelines. Each post was amply provided with support weapons: in some cases this might have surpassed the normal allocation of battalion support weapons such as heavy, medium and light machine guns, rocket launchers, automatic grenade launchers, mortars, anti-aircraft guns, for use against both aircraft and ground targets, and Stinger MANPADs.[3] In addition, storage dumps of ammunition, rations and other stores were established and a large number of anti-personnel mines were laid. Estimates for the intruders' force size vary but in May 1999, estimates varied between 800 and 1,000. This increased to 2,000 later on and subsequently to estimates of a full brigade of NLI supported by SSG and Mujahidin. The extent of the intrusion varied from an average four to five kilometres to a maximum of seven to eight kilometres.

Detection

Initial Indian Army patrols conducting routine surveillance detected intruders atop ridges during the period 8 to 15 May 1999.[4] Quite early on, the infiltration pattern suggested the participation of regular Pakistani troops as well as that of the Islamist militants. The scale of the infiltration was initially underestimated but it soon became clear that India was facing a major military incursion.

Lieutenant-General Rodrigues of the Indian Army during a visit to Siachen in the early 1990s. (Indian Army)

Control of the Kargil Sector on the Indian side rested on the shoulders of a solitary infantry brigade. 121 Independent (I) Infantry Brigade, with its headquarters at Kargil, was responsible for all operations in the Kargil Sector.[5] This brigade group formed part of the 3rd Infantry Division which was headquartered at Leh and which was responsible for operations in Ladakh. This included the 140km long stretch of the LoC in Kargil district up to NJ 9842, along the 110km long Actual Ground Position Line (AGPL) at Siachen Glacier plus along the Line of Actual Control (LAC) against China. This infantry brigade was a relatively small formation, with only three infantry battalions in its order of battle: indeed, when the dispositions of the 121 Infantry Brigade are studied closely, it is obvious that these included several large gaps in what were considered to be 'less threatened areas'.[6] The brigade was tasked with too much of a geographical responsibility and this ensured that the entire LoC as well as the AGPL could not be completely patrolled or protected, especially in winter and this contributed to the Pakistani success.

By the time of the Kargil War in 1999, both sides took immense care to equip the units involved in operations in the Siachen area with some of the best alpine gear available. This photograph shows a Pakistan Army soldier, fully outfitted for operations at high altitudes and in freezing cold temperatures. (Pakistan Army)

Pakistan Army Order of Battle

Pakistan has not quite fully admitted the role of its combat units during the Kargil Conflict and thus a detailed order of battle remains unavailable: indeed, much related information remains speculative. The burden of the Kargil campaign was borne by the Northern Light Infantry which is headquartered at Gilgit in Gilgit-Baltistan. Four battalions of the Northern Light Infantry Regiment – 5, 6, 8 and 12 NLI – were deployed in full strength, while elements of 3, 4, 7 and 11 NLI, together with the Chitral and Bajaur Scouts were employed for logistic support of the four combat units. These were under the control of 62 Brigade Pakistan Army and were provided with fire support from some 20 batteries of Pakistan Army artillery. Each NLI sub-unit involved in the infiltration was provided with lavish quantities of battalion level support weaponry and was well able to defend their positions with great tenacity against Indian assaults.[7]

Pakistan thus deployed an infantry- and artillery-dominated division-sized force during the Kargil War. This might not have committed all of its elements across the LoC, but the fact that infiltrators from the NLI had been assigned to brigade sectors speaks to the level of Pakistan Army support for the operation. In addition, the allocation of artillery was quite substantial for a brigade-level incursion with the equivalent of perhaps four full regiments of artillery plus three heavy mortar regiments being allocated to the task. This force was able to infiltrate across the Line of Control completely undetected and was able to occupy a number of ridgelines and heights, placing India's supply lines under threat with Pakistani artillery being quite astonishingly effective at interdicting Indian supply efforts, though ultimately not succeeding.

India's Intent to Protect Its Interests

During the course of the Kargil operations, numerous infantry battalions rotated through different brigades and were attached and detached as needed. For example, the Brigade of the Guards provided additional detachments with MILAN ATGMs which were used in the direct fire mode. Special forces units as well as India's counterinsurgency force, the Rashtriya Rifles, were also participants in the Kargil operations, with the Border Security Force and Central Reserve Police Force – which were part of the Central Armed Police Forces – supported the Army and helped preserve the integrity of the counterinsurgency grid that was critical to internal security in the state of Jammu and Kashmir.

No fewer than 19 artillery regiments participated in the war, attached to the artillery brigades of the respective divisions, XV Corps or independent units assigned to fire support. Field regiments were equipped with 105mm Indian Field Guns or Light Field Guns, medium regiments were equipped with 130mm M-46 guns and 155mm FH-77/B-02 Bofors Howitzers. Light regiments operated 120mm mortars while the sole heavy mortar regiment deployed fielded Tampella 160mm mortars. Some 75/24mm Indian-designed pack howitzers were used in the direct fire role while a rocket regiment with BM-21 122mm rockets was also deployed.

The deployment of artillery was lavish by Indian standards with some 3-400 artillery pieces and mortars in action to support Indian operations. This in turn placed a significant strain on India's ability to keep guns supplied with ammunition and spare parts. The use of older weapons was slowly discouraged with the 75/24mm gun being one which might have been deemed suitable for use in mountains: however, its short range and light shell were less than effective. This also applied, albeit to a lesser extent, to the 105mm field guns which were given less priority than larger calibre weapons.

The artillery units were supported by two Reconnaissance and Observation squadrons (663 and 668) of the Army Aviation Corps, both equipped with HAL Cheetah helicopters, a license-built Aérospatiale SE.315 Alouette II. These helicopters, in the absence of UAVs were to prove extremely valuable to the Indian Army. Not only did they provide excellent spotting for the artillery, but they also proved to be highly effective reconnaissance assets. While the helicopters initially flew with no sensor arrays of any kind, the Indian Army did experiment with fitting the FLIR turret of the Nishant UAV to the Cheetah helicopter to dramatically improve its night and bad weather surveillance capabilities. However, even with such equipment, the Cheetah remained a small and relatively vulnerable vehicle, and it is almost surprising that none was shot down.

The Indian Army's Corps of Air Defence Artillery also deployed units during the Kargil Conflict with P-18 radars and the 326th Light Air Defence Regiment (Composite) being deployed to give active support to the Indian Army in the event of any Pakistani air threat. Being a composite regiment, the 326th operated a combination of towed 23mm ZU-23-2 anti-aircraft guns and Igla-1M missiles and were assigned to defend artillery positions and to cover troop and munition convoys moving into the theatre. Additional support was provided by the Bofors L/70 40mm guns of the 323rd Air Defence Regiment which provided cover for vital areas and points, and the 146th Light Air Defence Regiment (Self-Propelled) which operated ZU-23-2 guns on 6x6 trucks.

Indian military operations continued from 12 May for seven weeks as New Delhi accepted neither ceasefire requests nor any efforts towards conciliation or negotiations. On the contrary, despite significant difficulties, its armed forces moved inexorably towards evicting the intruders.

Indian losses during the Kargil campaign were heavy. These included 26 Officers, 21 JCOs and 452 other ranks killed; 66 Officers, 60 JCOs and 1,085 other ranks wounded plus four missing for a total Indian casualty count of 1,714 killed, wounded and missing.[8] Materially, the IAF also lost one MiG-21M, one MiG-27L and one Mi-17, five Indian aircrew being killed in the process.

Pakistani losses were somewhat less clear, primarily because it took years for Islamabad to ever admit the involvement of its armed forces. Indian military intelligence estimated a total of 772 killed (including 69 Officers and 76 SSG personnel), over 1,000 wounded and eight POWs. Troops in contact with the Pakistanis suggest 597 killed while radio intercepts identified 591 killed. Prisoners included Naik Inayat Ali and Sepoys Hunar Shah, Sher Baz Khan and Mohammad Ayaz from 5 NLI; Sepoy Fazal Aman from 24 Sindh, Sepoys Abdul Hamid and Salik Khan from 33 Frontier Force Regiment and Sepoy Ashraf from 19 Frontier Force Regiment.[9] In addition, a number of diaries and identity documents were captured from Pakistani bodies which established the units from which many of the infiltrators originated. This undoubtedly helped India's narrative that the incursion was the work of Pakistani regulars rather than merely Pakistani-supported Mujahidin and served to bolster India's efforts.

Pakistan itself never admitted to the casualties suffered and even now only tangentially accepts that their troops were involved. Pervez Musharraf suggested 357 killed and 665 wounded; Nawaz Sharif's PML-N gives casualties of 3,000 Mujahidin, officers and soldiers of the NLI 'rendering sacrifice'; while the Pakistan Army named 453 killed in the Batalik-Kargil sector in 1999.[10]

Several Pakistani soldiers were later rewarded with decorations – some posthumously – such as Captain Karnal Sher and Major Iqbal. However, as the Pakistan Army was more than a little reluctant to acknowledge its role in sparking and then encouraging the conflict, many deserving Pakistani soldiers were not accorded due recognition for their sacrifices in a losing conflict. Rather more seriously for Pakistan is the continuing failure to hold senior officers responsible for initiating the conflict and then leaving a brigade sized formation to fend for itself against a determined Indian effort, ultimately successful, to dislodge and repel them.

Kargil War in Siachen

However, one part of the conflict remained largely unknown until sometime after the conclusion of hostilities. These were the operations conducted by 27 Rajput in the Turtuk southern glacier area, perhaps saving the Shyok River Valley and in turn the security of the Thoise airfield and the wider Nubra Valley. Had this operation not been undertaken, it is possible that India's hold on the Siachen Glacier and the Saltoro Ridge might have proven to be rather more precarious. The Battle for Navdeep Top, also called Point 5770, was an audacious attempt, far from the media and scrutiny of the press and even politicians, it was sharp but short and had an impact out of all proportions to the actual fighting that took place.

During the Kargil Conflict, the 102 Infantry Brigade – the Siachen Brigade – had a wide area of responsibility and had two sub-sectors assigned to it:

- Sub-Sector West (SSW): From Chorbatla, 18km due east to the River Shyok

An Indian soldier with INSAS assault rifle, seen during a patrol at Siachen Glacier in 1999. (Indian Army)

A group of Indian Army troops climbing the side of the Siachen Glacier, under conditions similar to those experienced by Major Cheema's troops on 27 June 1999. (Indian Army)

- Sub-Sector Hanif (SSH): From Turtok to a point 10km south-east of the southern glacier.[11]

The brigade was reinforced with additional infantry battalions and comprised 11 Raj Rif, 9 Mahar, 13 Kumaon, 27 Rajput, 5 Vikas and one company of the Ladakh Scouts to which were later added 3 Rajput. This made the 102 Infantry Brigade, still nominally under the command of 3 Infantry Division, one of the largest brigades in the Indian Army. The force also had an additional ATGM detachment from the 19th Battalion of the Brigade of the Guards, plus a detachment of specialised mountaineers and ski troops from HAWS which were permanently attached to the 102 Infantry Brigade to provide specialised assistance in Siachen military operations.[12]

In June 1999, 27 Rajput, joined by Major Navdeep Singh Cheema and Captain Shyamal Sinha of 9 Kumaon and who had recently been trained at HAWS and a team from the Ladakh Scouts prepared for their assault on Bilal Post – Point 5770.[13] This team had been extensively acclimatised and had also been trained at the Siachen Battle School. This made the team well prepared for the task they were about to undertake. As with so much of the Kargil operations, it was a small unit operation, dependent on training, skill and determination.

The team operated, initially, more like mountaineers, than as soldiers and established a clear route, fixing ropes along the way to enable following troops to climb the slopes more easily. However, extremely bad weather created some considerable havoc. An initial attempt on the night of 23-24 June, saw the troops start the climb but had to abort owing to a blizzard blowing across the area and deteriorating conditions as dawn was about to break, the assault was called off. Once again, as so often is the case in Siachen, weather was a major operational factor.[14]

A second attempt, on 25 June was attempted in daylight but this proved to be very time consuming and the teams got within 50 feet of the objective when Major Cheema decided that the conditions did not warrant the risk of a night attack and opted to call off the attack, especially considering the combination of weather and a paucity of night-vision equipment that plagued the Indian Army throughout most of the Kargil Conflict. The two assaulting columns were recalled, and a fresh team was selected for the third and ultimately decisive Indian assault.[15]

At 3.00hrs on 27 June, the third assault began. Major Cheema and Captain Sinha led a team of 27 Rajput and after 11 hours of arduous climbing, the first assault team reached its objective. There was little by way of resistance and Captain Taimur Malik and 10 soldiers of 3 NLI were killed with the 27 Rajput suffering no losses. As a result of this action, Bilal Post was renamed Navdeep Post by the Indian Army. No further fighting was reported in the Siachen sector.

The Kargil Endgame

As might be expected, the Pakistani government approached the United States of America for assistance in bringing the conflict to an end. Prime Minister Nawaz Sharif became increasingly desperate as realisation dawned at the extent of Pakistan's isolation in respect of the Kargil Conflict. Efforts to involve the G8 and UN after some calls for dialogue, ended with no positive result for Pakistan.[16] This led to Pakistan placing its hopes in the United States. At the same time, India's Prime Minister, Atal Bihari Vajpayee, was absolutely resolute in his view that nothing could be entertained short of a Pakistani withdrawal. To this end, Pakistani Prime Minister Sharif, urgently requested American intervention to stop the Indian counterattack. However, Washington was adamant and consistent in its approach that any solution required a Pakistani withdrawal behind the LoC and nothing short of that would suffice.[17]

A Mi-17 helicopter of the Indian Air Force loading supplies for the troops deployed on the Siachen Glacier. The terrain and weather are so inhospitable that containers are frequently air-dropped, instead of the helicopters attempting a landing to unload. (IAF)

A Mi-17 (serial number Z3009) paradropping supplies for the Indian troops on the Siachen Glacier in 1999. (Indian Army)

As the Indian counteroffensive continued, in the last days of June Sharif began to ask to visit President Clinton and to directly plead his case for US intervention. On 2 July Sharif made a call to Clinton where he appealed for American intervention to stop the fighting and to resolve the Kashmir issue. In contrast, President Clinton was very explicit in his view that he could help only if Pakistan first withdrew to its side of the LoC. The President also consulted with Indian Prime Minister Vajpayee who was adamant that India would not negotiate under the threat of aggression and that Pakistan needed to withdraw across the LoC.[18]

On 3 July 1999, Sharif was even more desperate and told President Clinton he was ready to come to Washington immediately to seek help. The US President repeated his view that Sharif should only come if Pakistan was ready to withdraw and that no help could be forthcoming if Pakistan did not withdraw. Despite this, Sharif travelled to Washington, a day later. In the course of a meeting with Clinton, he attempted to plead the cause of Kashmiri separatism, Pakistan's claim on the territory and to press for external intervention to 'solve' the problem. However, Clinton refused to be persuaded by such arguments and instead insisted on a Pakistani withdrawal. After much debate and consultation, an increasingly desperate Sharif agreed to a draft statement.

This statement paved the way for an end to hostilities with Pakistani troops withdrawing behind the LoC and India reoccupying all posts hitherto unoccupied by its forces. Indian assets monitored the Pakistani withdrawal and verified the repositioning of the intruding forces to behind the Line of Control.[19]

The Kargil Conflict was South Asia's first post-nuclear war and one which showed the real limits of nuclear deterrence. Both sides lost hundreds of personnel, India's treated as heroes, Pakistan's forgotten in a losing effort. Pakistan learned that the international community would not diplomatically intervene to a limited Indian response. India's resolve in the face of military adventurism was underestimated by Pakistan to its cost.

It is difficult to overstate the impact of the Kargil War on the Indian psyche and on its concerns for the supply routes for the Siachen Brigade. This conflict involved a significant number of troops on the Indian side and, inadvertently, owing to other commitments, allowed China to make inroads into certain areas in Ladakh in the region of Pangong Tso. The conflict was brisk, bloody and very expensive in lives, materiel and money. It directly led to the fall of the Pakistani government and the re-election of India's – all because of India's concerns for its Siachen and Saltoro holdings.

India's hold on Siachen and the audacity of Operation Meghdoot at least at some level factored into Pakistan's planning for Operation Badr and the wider Kargil War. However, the Pakistanis, despite achieving complete surprise and securing the peaks of Kargil and being able to interdict India's supply lines, completely underestimated India's resolve, its determination not to capitulate and its intention not to allow its supply lines to Siachen to be compromised or threatened in any way. In this regard, Pakistan found itself in an unwinnable situation and, given India's willingness to sustain casualties in the process, inevitably lost the Kargil War.

Perhaps the final word on the Kargil Conflict should be left to retired Lt. General Shahid Aziz, former Chief of General Staff of the Pakistan Army: 'It was a failure because we had to hide its objectives and results from our own people and the nation. It had no purpose, no planning and nobody knows even today how many soldiers lost their lives.'[20]

Kargil and Siachen are inextricably linked, as is the broader history of conflict between India and Pakistan and India and China. Military forces deployed by India and Pakistan have therefore evolved to cater for their perceived threats and geostrategic interests and vulnerabilities and, consequently, have both similarities and differences. The Kargil War, however, was to bring about a period of relative calm in the region with neither side initiating major military action.

7
SIACHEN IN THE 21ST CENTURY

Survival at the Top of the World

Fighting on the Siachen Glacier has been nearly non-existent since the beginning of the 21st century. However, in a conflict where over 1,100 Indian soldiers have been killed, and an unknown number of Pakistanis, it might not be surprising to note that the majority of the casualties suffered in the conflict have been due to medical conditions and avalanches.[1] Both sides make extensive use of troop rotation and helicopters to supply their forces and to ensure that soldiers stationed on the glacier are not allowed to be completely worn out. It is a conflict that has exacted a high price in monetary terms but also in terms of lives. Yet, it has also hardened both armies in perhaps the toughest battlefield on the planet.

Medical Care

The conditions that the Indian and Pakistani armies face have not changed since Operation Meghdoot started the Siachen conflict. However, what has dramatically changed are the medical facilities available to support the troops. India's Army Medical Corps, for example, has dramatically enhanced the survival rate of troops facing the extreme altitude and cold conditions of the Siachen Glacier. This means that soldiers who had little chance of survival now have a fighting chance and death rates on both sides have improved quite dramatically over the years.

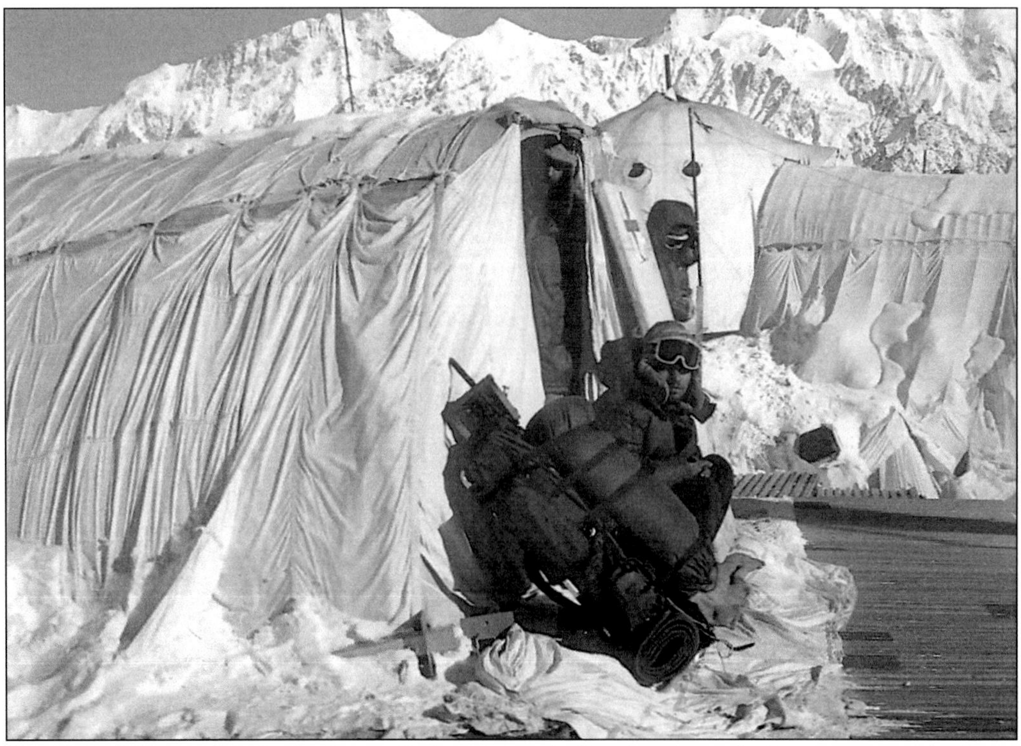

A regimental aid post of the Indian Army in Siachen: always the first place for medical treatment of any kind. (Indian Army)

One Indian Army doctor, noting the extreme conditions and the challenges facing his profession, stated:

The human body makes adjustments in its functioning to enable individuals to live and work at extreme altitudes. These adjustments continue the phenomenon of altitude acclimatization. Acclimatization, which largely involves increase in the rate and depth of breathing, and increase in haemoglobin levels in the blood, however, does not allow the human body to function on Siachen as it does at sea level. At an altitude of 5,000 metres, for example, the levels of oxygen in the blood of a healthy soldier would be similar to that of a patient with a severe lung disorder at sea level. While such patients are admitted to ICUs, confined to beds and treated with continuous oxygen therapy, and soldiers at 5,000 metres with similar levels of oxygen in their blood perform intense physical activity and fight the enemy.[2]

Quick evacuation is of crucial importance for any casualties in Siachen: this is where helicopters play an important role. (Indian Army)

In recent years, Indian Army troops have used snowmobiles to patrol the crisis zone: this group was photographed near the northern edge of the Siachen Glacier. (Indian Army)

High Altitude Pulmonary Oedema (HAPO) used to affect some 15 out of every hundred soldiers who served on Siachen. Improvements in training and medical care have meant that this figure is now less than one in 100. Deaths from HAPO, which were a common occurrence in the 1980s and 1990s, have now been reduced to a rarity.[3] This has been done through the use of HAPO bags and rapid evacuation to medical facilities through improved helicopters such as the HAL Dhruv Mk III which have excellent high altitude capabilities and are able to operate with a useful payload.

However, casualty evacuation and medical care for wounded soldiers is still a major challenge. Despite the availability of significant helicopter assets, the inclement weather and the lack of landing sites as such, some of the initial evacuation is done by foot. One doctor recalled:

> Improvisations and presence of mind makes the difference between life and death. As a young medical officer, I recall the day we suffered three casualties due to enemy shelling. As we watched our OP [observation post] came under artillery fire, there was little we could do but hope for the best. A call on the radio set confirmed our worst fears. Three soldiers were wounded with multiple splinter injuries. The wait for the shelling to stop was agonizing. I was desperate to know how much was the blood loss. As night fell and we were permitted to move, we asked a neighbouring post to begin evacuating the wounded down towards us, and we set off towards them trying to meet the wounded halfway, so that they could be treated as quickly as possible. We met an hour later, on the vast desolate openness of the glacier. Under muffled torch lights, a quick examination of the wounded revealed that they needed pain relief on priority. It was perhaps the most difficult injection that I have ever administered to a patient. At 17,000 feet, and sub-zero temperature, the vast emptiness of the glacier, the sky as our roof and the threat of fresh enemy fire, that was the place where I treated the injured! We brought the casualties to the company base using skid boards as ice sleighs and parachute strings as harnesses, sliding them over the glacier, taking turns every few minutes to ensure we did not tire ourselves. The night was spent in our tent using kerosene

> stoves to provide warmth. We sang songs to keep our wounded friends awake, joking how they would have pretty nurses looking after them in a few hours' time. Silently we prayed for clear weather the next morning to permit an early evacuation.[4]

Unfortunately, medical attention and care cannot assist with avalanches which routinely bury entire patrols in a single swoop. While significant advances have been made in the sphere of avalanche search techniques, a single avalanche on 7 April 2012 killed 129 Pakistani soldiers and 11 Pakistani civilians.[5] Unfortunately, this was not an isolated event and both armies routinely suffer the loss of men through these acts of nature.

Equipment and Air Bridges

Cold weather gear has also dramatically improved though the cost is very high, with India estimating that the cost is approximately INR 100,000 per soldier:

> The most expensive part of the personal kit of soldiers includes the multi-layered extreme winter clothing which costs around Rs 28,000 per set along with the special sleeping bag which is worth around Rs 13,000.
>
> The down jacket and the special gloves of troops together cost around Rs 14,000 while the multipurpose shoes cost around Rs 12,500.
>
> Of the equipment provided to the troops, the oxygen cylinder costs Rs 50,000 per piece which is very important at those altitudes as the oxygen levels are very low there.
>
> The soldiers also get equipment and gadgets for detecting avalanche victims which costs around Rs 8,000.[6]

Despite these expenses, there are always concerns about shortages of equipment. India has made an effort to indigenise equipment but Pakistan's army continues to complain about conditions and equipment compared to the Indians.[7]

Helicopter support has improved considerably from the days of 1984, at least on the Indian side. Pakistan's helicopter fleet, as noted in the relevant chapter, still relies on Pumas, Mi-17s and Alouette II helicopters for support. In India's case, a force of Mi-17s operates from Leh, Thoise and Base Camp Siachen while a force of Cheetahs from 114 HU and two other helicopter units, including one of HAL Dhruv Mk.III helicopters, are on permanent duty ferrying supplies.[8] Air support is absolutely essential, as described by Lt. General Syed Ata Hasnain of 4 Garhwal:

> On the northern glacier, there are no porters. All the haulage is done by soldiers. The drops used to begin early in the morning. That time [in the mid-nineties], kerosene jerry cans, apart from the heavy stuff needed for heating used to be dropped by Mi-17s and AN-32s through orange or red coloured parachutes, as near to the posts as possible. At the posts there was an entire arrangement to keep a close eye on the drops. Once the Mi-17s and the transport aircraft had departed, work for the ground soldiers would begin. They would fan out to the spots already noted, some on snow scooters, most on foot, roped to each other, locate the parachutes, haul the loads on sledges, tie them up to the snow scooters or start pulling them to their pre-determined storage points. That is the time the soldiers were most dangerous to crevasses, especially in summer months when they open up in large numbers.[9]

Life on the glacier is nightmarish in most respects and basic supplies freeze solid in the temperatures. An Indian journalist

A Mi-17 (serial Z-3377) approaching a forward base on the Siachen Glacier. (IAF)

who visited the Siachen Glacier noted:

> In such an extreme environment, normal life is virtually impossible because almost everything freezes solid: onions are [hard] to cut, eggs become like rocks and cannot even be broken and most toothpaste (except gels) cannot be squeezed out. Chocolates become as hard as steel plates and if you bite them, you could break your teeth.
>
> Metal and the human skin become so chilled that when a jawan tries to load his gun, the bullets stick to his gloveless hand. If he tries to take them off, the skin will also peel off. One Siachen trooper told us: "Except for rum and kerosene, everything is frozen solid."
>
> Soldiers who have stayed on the Saltoro peaks during winter confessed that they were never entirely warm. "Even with all your down clothing, you cannot stand outside for more than 10 minutes…"
>
> Almost all the food on the glacier comes in tins. And despite the wide variety available, it all tastes the same. "We are all dying to see and eat anything fresh and green," says one Mahar officer. Cooking rice and Dal takes hours in the rarefied atmosphere.
>
> For extra nourishment troops are issued special rations: cream biscuits, fruit juice, chocolates, almonds, cashew-nuts and cheese. But most of these are alien to the palate of the rustic jawan, who treats chocolates and biscuits with total disdain.
>
> In fact, at some of the forward posts, the jawans have used chocolate slabs to make stairs, while biscuit packets were stacked up to make bunkers. The authorities, keen on pumping the troops with additional calories, have devised unique recipes.
>
> Thus the Siachen *halwa* is a concoction of mashed biscuits, chocolate powder, dry fruits, and milk mixed with *sooji* and *ghee*. Or the Siachen omelette: an omelette wrapped around steaming Maggi noodles.
>
> But despite such innovations, the jawans lose their appetite and can shed up to 12kg during their tour of duty.[10]

In recent years, the Indian Army has primarily deployed its HAL Dhruv utility helicopters for supporting troops on the Siachen Glacier. Developed by Hindustan Aeronautics Limited with assistance from MBB in Germany, the type entered service in 2002: by October 2020, more than 300 have been manufactured. (Indian Army)

While some items have improved considerably and support and logistics are more equal to the task, there is little doubt that core conditions and imperatives have remained largely unchanged and soldiers assigned to duty on the Siachen Glacier face extremely difficult conditions. India has shown that it is intent on bearing this cost, for better or worse.

Troop rotation is extensive. India rotates no fewer than 12 infantry battalions through the glacier each year. In addition, supporting arms – engineers, artillery, signals, supply and medical – all have to rotate through a tour of duty. This means India deploys some 15,000 to 20,000 troops each year to the Siachen Glacier. Each of these soldiers has to be supplied, armed, trained and equipped for operations in inhospitable conditions and this, as has been shown, requires a huge logistics and resupply effort.

An FH-770B2 howitzer in position near the Siachen Glacier: they are used by the Indian Army for long-range fire support. (Indian Army)

With respect to new weapons, as described earlier, both armed forces have developed and honed their skills, their weapons have followed a more normal modernisation process with Pakistan, having the luxury of a one-front war, not having to develop the specialised mountain formations that India has had to create in order to deal with both its conflict with Pakistan and its threat from

A Dhruv helicopter of the Indian Army transporting a ZU-23-2 anti-aircraft gun to a new position on the Siachen Glacier. (Indian MOD)

China. However, its formations can be switched as needed to be brought to bear on either adversary as the need arises.

It is of interest to note, however, the Siachen troops were the first to receive Dragunov designated marksman rifles and automatic grenade launchers and, long before the Kargil Conflict of 1999, they and the Pakistanis, had made extensive use of ATGMs against bunkers – SS-11Bs for India and TOWs for Pakistan. India has brought up at least one battery of six Bofors 155mm FH-77B02 guns to the Siachen base camp while Pakistan uses a mix of vintage artillery – 3.7 inch mountain howitzers were in use into the 1990s – and modern pieces. These deployments continue to date. It should be noted, however, that the extreme environment has a serious impact on the performance of weapons with artillery range tables having to be re-written and usually reliable rifles – the old 7.62mm SLR for India and the G3 for Pakistan – having to be heated regularly to prevent them from freezing solid. The effects of ammunition are also magnified in these conditions with splinter effects being particularly enhanced with the attendant uncertainty produced by an inability to predict effects.[11]

It might be said that the Siachen Glacier has tested the two armies the way no other battlefield could possibly do. Yet, in 2003 a ceasefire was negotiated and an effort was made to find a solution. These efforts did not succeed.

No War but No Peace

Four years after the Kargil Conflict, a ceasefire came into effect on the Siachen Glacier and combat operations have not taken place since that date. The idea of demilitarising the Siachen Glacier has been floated since 1989, under the then Indian Prime Minister Rajiv Gandhi who was reeling under a number of political and internal security challenges. At the time, these proposals went nowhere and the fighting continued sporadically for another decade at varying levels of intensity. The ceasefire of 2003 was initially supposed to be precursor to a more permanent solution but this was not to be, though serious efforts were made between 2005 and 2012.[12]

In 2012, however, the two countries came very close to realising a deal on the Siachen Glacier and its demilitarisation. India was then under the leadership of Dr. Manmohan Singh who was anxious for a lasting peace with Pakistan and as part of his efforts, despite the challenges of Pakistani terror attacks – the 26 November 2008 assault on Mumbai was still very raw in the Indian psyche – he was prepared to make many compromises in the hope of securing some vestige of a peaceful settlement with his Pakistani counterparts.

On 13 June 2005, Dr. Singh while addressing Indian soldiers at the Siachen base camp, made a statement that was as clear a declaration of intent as was possible: 'Siachen is called the highest battlefield, where living is very difficult. Now the time has come that we make efforts that this is converted from a point of conflict to the symbol of peace.'[13]

However, as noted above, the periodic terror attacks from Pakistani based – and sponsored – terrorist groups and the trauma of the 2008 Mumbai attacks meant that progress was slow for several years. Having secured re-election in 2009, however, Dr. Singh's government was intent on achieving Siachen's demilitarisation during his tenure and he therefore authorised his Minister of Defence, A.K. Anthony, a close confidant of the influential Nehru

Gunners of the Indian Army with a ZU-23-2 anti-aircraft gun in position on the Siachen Glacier. (Indian MOD)

A Pakistan Army patrol in deep snow along the Line of Control. (Pakistan Army)

One of the most recently released photographs from the Siachen, showing Indian troops guiding a group of tourists along the glacier. (Indian MOD)

dynasts that controlled Dr. Singh's government, to initiate the modalities for India and Pakistan to begin discussions in earnest on achieving the demilitarisation of the Siachen Glacier with a mutual withdrawal of all forces.[14] These proposals were widely supported by members of the then Indian government though it was uncertain as to how much support there was in the public domain.

According to former Indian Foreign Secretary, Shyam Saran, there was apparently wide consensus on the need for a demilitarisation of Siachen and for the commencement of talks with Pakistan. Saran went so far as to suggest that a legally binding agreement with Pakistan had been worked out in early 2006, and had been prepared for the Indian Cabinet Committee on Security (CCS) which was the apex political decision-making body for all security matters in India. However, at this point, the then National Security Advisor, M.K. Narayan and the Indian Army Chief of Staff, General J. J. Singh, intervened:

> When the CCS meeting was held on the eve of the Defence Secretary-level talks, the NSA launched an offensive, saying that Pakistan could not be trusted, and that there will be political and public opposition to any such initiative and that India's military position in the northern sector vis-à-vis both Pakistan and China will be compromised. General Singh, who had happily gone along with the proposal in its earlier iterations, now decided to join Narayanan in rubbishing it…[15]

After this attempt, several more efforts were made to find some way of demilitarising the Siachen Glacier and these received a major impetus when Pakistan suffered a major non-military loss which was to shake its confidence as well as, it would appear, its political resolve. Pakistan's Army Chief, Ashfaq Pervez Kayani, following the tragedy of the 2012 avalanche that killed 140 Pakistanis, made a statement, once again pushing for demilitarisation:

> Both countries should sit together to resolve all the issues, including Siachen...Pakistan deployed its forces on the Siachen Glacier in response to the Indian occupation of a part of the glacier. The soldiers are doing their duty to defend the country and it is for the political leadership to find a solution.[16]

This was further enhanced by comments from Nawaz Sharif, Pakistan's former prime minister and Imran Khan, who would later become the country's Prime Minister, with military backing. The latter stated: 'Pakistan and India should simultaneously withdraw troops from Siachen.'[17]

However, it was then that India's then Chief of Army Staff, General V.K. Singh and his predecessors unanimously agitated against any Indian withdrawal from the Siachen Glacier, one source telling defence correspondents that:

> There is no reason for withdrawal from Siachen at this stage. Both tactically and strategically, holding those commanding heights is to India's advantage. Pakistan has given no reason for India to trust it. The Chief [V.K. Singh] is very clear in his mind. If ordered to withdraw troops, he would seek an order in writing and give his opinion that he opposes withdrawal in national interest in writing. After that, it is the Prime Minister's decision…[18]

Despite his own desire for the Siachen demilitarisation deal, Dr. Manmohan Singh was increasingly concerned about appearing to

A classic photograph of an Indian Army patrol underway on the Siachen. Their alpine gear, necessary to survive operations in this climate and altitude, they almost appear to be wearing space suits. (Indian Army)

be weak after his failure to respond strongly to the Mumbai attacks and the deep distrust that India had in respect of Pakistan's sincerity. This might seem to be somewhat short-sighted on India's part, perhaps even petty. However, time would prove India's generals to be correct in their assessment as a much more serious threat to Eastern Ladakh would emerge in 2020 when China began a series of incursions there.

Conclusion

India's War in Siachen has come to be both a symbolic military achievement as well as a practical and important strategic objective. As noted in the first chapter of this book, India's hold on the Siachen Glacier and the Saltoro Ridge gives it the ability to interdict the Karakoram Highway and to prevent any effective joint military operation by both Pakistan and China. As tensions in Eastern Ladakh were increased in 2020 and India and China each massed some 50,000 troops in theatre with tanks, artillery, airpower and missiles, India's 102 Infantry Brigade and its Siachen mission is now essential.

BIBLIOGRAPHY

Ahluwaia V. K. and Singh, N., (ed.) *Surprise, Strategy and "Vijay": 20 Years of Kargil and Beyond* (New Delhi: Centre for Land Warfare Studies, 2019)

Badri-Maharaj, S., *The Armageddon Factor: Nuclear Weapons in the India-Pakistan Context* (New Delhi: Lancer, 2000)

Badri-Maharaj, S., *Kargil 1999: South Asia's Post-Nuclear Conflict* (Warwick: Helion & Co, 2020)

Bajpai, K., Chari, P., Cheema, P., Cohen, S., Ganguly, S., (ed.), *Brasstacks and Beyond: Perception and Management of Crisis in South Asia* (New Delhi: Manohar, 1995)

Brar, K. S., *Operation Blue Star: The True Story* (New Delhi: UBSPD, 1993)

Conboy, Kenneth, *Elite Forces of India and Pakistan* (London: Osprey Military, 1992)

Fontanellaz, A. & Cooper, T., *Paradise Afire, Volume 1: The Sri Lankan War, 1971-1987* (Solihull: Helion & Co., 2018)

Fontanellaz, A., *Paradise Afire, Volume 2: The Sri Lankan War, 1987-1990* (Warwick: Helion & Co., 2019)

Fontanellaz, A., *Paradise Afire, Volume 3: The Sri Lankan War, 1990-1994* (Warwick: Helion & Co., 2020)

Gokhale, N. A., *Beyond NJ9842: the Siachen Saga* (New Delhi: Bloomsbury, 2015)

Joshi, M., *The Lost Rebellion: Kashmir in the Nineties* (New Delhi: Penguin, 1999)

Kanwal, G., *Kargil '99: Blood Guts and Firepower* (New Delhi: Lancer, 2000)

Kanwal, G., 'Pakistan's Strategic Blunder at Kargil', *CLAWS Journal*, Summer 2009

Kapadia Harish, *Siachen Glacier: The Battle of Roses.* (New Delhi: Rupa Publications Pvt. Ltd. 2010)

Khanna, D.K., *Gorichen to Siachen* (New Delhi: Alpha Editions, 2017)

Krishna, A., (ed.), *Kargil: The Tables Turned* (New Delhi: Manohar, 2001)

Lambeth, B., *Airpower at 18,000: The Indian Air Force in the Kargil War* (Washington DC: Carnegie Endowment for International Peace, 2012)

Malik, V. P., *Kargil: From Surprise to Victory* (New Delhi: Harper Collins, 2009)

Malik, V. P., 'The Kargil War: Some Reflections', *CLAWS Journal*, Summer 2009

Nasim, Z., *From Kargil to Coup: Events that Shook Pakistan* (Lahore: Sang-e-Meel, 2018)

Pakistan Army's Misadventure in Kargil (New Delhi: Army Liaison Cell, Army Headquarters, 1999)

Perkovich, G., *India's Nuclear Bomb: The Impact on Global Proliferation* (London: University of California Press, 1999)

Prasad, S. N. (ed.), *Operations in Jammu & Kashmir, 1947-48* (New Delhi: Natraj, 2005)

Prasad, S. N., Thapliyal, U. P. (ed.), *The India-Pakistan War of 1965* (New Delhi: Natraj, 2011)

Prasad, S. N., Thapliyal, U. P. (ed.), *The India-Pakistan War of 1971* (New Delhi: Natraj, 2014)

Puri, M., *Kargil: Turning the Tide* (New Delhi: Lancer, 2016)

Qadir, Shaukat, 'An Analysis of the Kargil Conflict 1999', *RUSI Journal*, April 2002

Rikhye, R,. Singh, P., Steinemann, P., *Fiza'Ya: Psyche of the Pakistan Air Force* (New Delhi: S. A. S., 1991)

Rikhye, R., *Indo-Pakistan War of 1971, Volume 1: Indian Military Intervention in East Pakistan* (Warwick: Helion & Co., 2020)

Sawant, G., *Dateline Kargil* (New Delhi: MacMillan, 2000)

Singh, Amarinder, *A Ridge Too Far: War in the Kargil Heights 1999* (Patiala: Motibag Palace, 2001)

The Kargil Review Committee Report: From Surprise to Reckoning (New Delhi: Sage, 1999)

Tufail, K., *Against All Odds: Pakistan Air Force in the 1971 India-Pakistan War* (Warwick: Helion & Co., 2020)

Tufail, K., 'Role of the Pakistan Air Force During the Kargil Conflict', *CLAWS Journal*, Summer 2009

Verma, K. & Williams, R. *The Long Road to Siachen: The Question Why* (New Delhi: Rupa Publications, 2010)

NOTES

Chapter 1

1 Nitin A Gokhale, *Beyond NJ 9842: The SIACHEN Saga* (New Delhi: Bloomsbury Publishing, 2015), p.364.
2 Desmond/Kashmir, Edward W. (31 July 1989). "The Himalayas War at the Top of the World". *Time*. Archived from the original on 14 January 2009. Retrieved 11 October 2008.
3 India gained control over Siachen in 1984". *Times of India*. Retrieved 4 August 2017.
4 Dinesh Kumar (13 April 2014). "30 Years of the World's Coldest War". *The Tribune*. Chandigarh, India. Retrieved 18 April 2014.
5 Feryal Ali Gauhar, Ahmed Yusuf, "Siachen: The place of wild roses". *Dawn*. 2 November 2014. Retrieved 4 August 2017.
6 D.K. Khanna, *Gorichen to Siachen: The Untold Saga of Hoisting the Tricolour on Saltoro* (New Delhi: Alpha Editions, 2017), p.34.
7 Khanna, p.34.
8 Khanna, pp.34-35
9 Khanna, pp.34-35
10 Khanna, p.39
11 Khanna, p.40
12 Khanna, p.41
13 For details on the Kargil War, see Badri-Maharaj, *Kargil 1999*
14 Gokhale, *Beyond NJ 9842*, p.16

Chapter 2

1 For a detailed account, a good starting point is Prasad (ed.), *Operations in Jammu & Kashmir 1947-48*
2 UN Security Council Resolution 47:The India-Pakistan Question
3 UN Security Council Resolution 47:The India-Pakistan Question
4 See S.N Prasad and UP Thapliyal ed, *The India-Pakistan War of 1965* (Natraj: New Delhi: 2011)
5 Prasad et al, *The India-Pakistan War of 1965*
6 Text of Tashkent Declaration (as available at https://mea.gov.in)
7 Prasad et al, *The India-Pakistan War of 1971*
8 For a detailed reconstruction of the 1971 India-Pakistan War, see Rikhye, *The Indo-Pakistani War of 1971, Volume 1* & Tufail, *Against all Odds*
9 Simla Agreement July 2, 1972 (as available at https://mea.gov.in)
10 "Line of Actual Control remains sore point between India and China", *India Today*, 18 May 1998, https://www.indiatoday.in/magazine/cover-story/story/19980518-line-of-actual-control-remains-sore-point-between-india-and-china-826413-1998-05-18
11 See K.S. Brar, *Operation Blue Star – The True Story* (UBSPD: New Delhi: 1993). For an account of the early years of the Kashmir insurgency, see Manoj Joshi, *The Lost Rebellion: Kashmir in the Nineties* (Penguin: New Delhi 1999)

Chapter 3

1 Sanjay Badri-Maharaj, *The Armageddon Factor: Nuclear Weapons in the India-Pakistan Context* (New Delhi: Lancer, 2000), pp.169–190
2 The L4A4 itself was a slightly modernized version of the Second World War vintage Bren Gun rechambered to fire the 7.62mm NATO round.
3 Sanjay Badri-Maharaj "Mountain Divisions a Work in Progress" *Geopolitics,* January 2019, pp.32-37
4 Badri-Maharaj "Mountain Divisions a Work in Progress", pp.32-37
5 Sanjay Badri-Maharaj "India's Military Special Forces" *Geopolitics,* November 2019, pp.18-23
6 Badri-Maharaj "India's Military Special Forces", pp.18-23
7 Badri-Maharaj "India's Military Special Forces", pp.18-23
8 Conboy, pp.14-21
9 Conboy, pp.14-21
10 Rajat Pandit "High-altitude Warfare School takes Global Aim" *Times of India* May 1 2004 https://timesofindia.indiatimes.com/india/High-altitude-warfare-school-takes-global-aim/articleshow/651951.cms
11 Deepshiksha Hooda, "High-Altitude Warfare School: Where Indian Jawans are taught to Survive in Siachen" *Economic Times*, July 11 2018, https://economictimes.indiatimes.com/news/defence/high-altitude-warfare-school-where-indian-jawans-are-trained-to-survive-in-siachen/articleshow/50968653.cms
12 Badri-Maharaj, *The Armageddon Factor*, pp.169–190
13 Badri-Maharaj, *The Armageddon Factor*, pp.169–190
14 Badri-Maharaj, *The Armageddon Factor*, pp.169–190
15 Badri-Maharaj, *The Armageddon Factor*, pp.169–190
16 Sanjay Badri-Maharaj, *Kargil 1999 – South Asia's First Post-Nuclear Conflict* (Warwick: Helion, 2020), pp.50-51
17 Syed Ishfaq Ali, *Fangs of Ice: The Story of Siachen* (New Delhi: Pak American Commercial), p.161
18 https://www.youtube.com/watch?v=pweZWZzPSk0 accessed January 2019 (video now deleted)
19 Ravi Rikhye, *The War that Never Was* (New Delhi: Chanakya Publications, 1988), pp.137-141
20 Rikhye, *The War that Never Was,* pp.137-141
21 Rikhye, *The War that Never Was,* pp.137-141
22 Rikhye, *The War that Never Was,* pp.137-141
23 Sanjay Badri-Maharaj, "It's Not just About Combat Aircraft", *Geopolitics,* October 2019, pp.26-30
24 Badri-Maharaj, "It's Not just About Combat Aircraft", pp.26-30
25 Badri-Maharaj, "It's Not just About Combat Aircraft", pp.26-30
26 Badri-Maharaj, "It's Not just About Combat Aircraft", pp.26-30
27 Badri-Maharaj, "It's Not just About Combat Aircraft", pp.26-30
28 Badri-Maharaj "Mountain Divisions a Work in Progress", pp.32-37
29 A.K. Tiwary, *Indian Air Force in Wars* (New Delhi: Lancer, 2012), pp.314-320
30 Rikhye, *The War that Never Was,* pp.137-141
31 Rikhye, *The War that Never Was,* pp.137-141
32 Rikhye, *The War that Never Was,* pp.137-141
33 Rikhye, *The War that Never Was,* pp.137-141
34 Sanjay Badri-Maharaj, "The Indian Air Force at 86: Options and Challenges" *Vayu Aerospace and Defence Review V/2018,* pp.37-41
35 Badri-Maharaj, "The Indian Air Force at 86: Options and Challenges", pp.37-41
36 Badri-Maharaj, "The Indian Air Force at 86: Options and Challenges", pp.37-41
37 Badri-Maharaj, "The Indian Air Force at 86: Options and Challenges", pp.37-41
38 "MiG-29"https://bharatrakshak.fandom.com/wiki/MiG-29
39 "Pakistan claims its fighter jets flew near Siachen, India says no airspace violation" https://economictimes.indiatimes.com/news/defence/pakistan-claims-its-fighter-jets-flew-near-siachen-india-says-no-airspace-violation/articleshow/58822096.cms

Chapter 4

1 Gokhale, *Beyond NJ 9842,* p.ix
2 Gokhale, *Beyond NJ 9842,* p.12
3 Gokhale, *Beyond NJ 9842,* p.13
4 Gokhale, *Beyond NJ 9842,* p.13
5 Gokhale, *Beyond NJ 9842,* pp.14-17
6 Gokhale, *Beyond NJ 9842,* pp.14-17
7 Colonel N. Kumar & Colonel N.N. Bhatia, *Soldier Mountaineer: The Colonel who got Siachen Glacier for India* (New Delhi: Vij Books, 2016), pp.192-200
8 Gokhale, *Beyond NJ 9842,* pp.23-30
9 Gokhale, *Beyond NJ 9842,* p.33
10 Gokhale, *Beyond NJ 9842,* p.34
11 Gokhale, *Beyond NJ 9842,* pp.34-35
12 Khanna, *Gorichen to Siachen,* p.14
13 Khanna, *Gorichen to Siachen,* p.14
14 Khanna, *Gorichen to Siachen,* p.14
15 Khanna, *Gorichen to Siachen,* p.16
16 Khanna, *Gorichen to Siachen,* p.17
17 Khanna, *Gorichen to Siachen,* p.18
18 Kumar & Bhatia, *Soldier Mountaineer*, pp.36-37
19 Kumar & Bhatia, p.37
20 Kumar & Bhatia, p.37
21 Kumar & Bhatia, pp.38-39
22 Kumar & Bhatia, p.38
23 Kumar & Bhatia, p.43
24 Kumar & Bhatia, pp.43-44
25 Kumar & Bhatia, pp.43-44
26 Kumar & Bhatia, p.40
27 Kumar & Bhatia, p.40
28 Quoted in Gokhale, *Beyond NJ 9842*, pp.42-43
29 Gokhale, *Beyond NJ 9842*, pp.42-43
30 Gokhale, *Beyond NJ 9842*, pp.42-43
31 Gokhale, *Beyond NJ 9842*, pp.48-49
32 Gokhale, *Beyond NJ 9842*, pp.48-49
33 Gokhale, *Beyond NJ 9842*, pp.48-49
34 Gokhale, *Beyond NJ 9842*, p.50
35 Gokhale, *Beyond NJ 9842*, p.50
36 Gokhale, *Beyond NJ 9842*, p.51
37 Gokhale, *Beyond NJ 9842*, pp.51-52
38 Gokhale, *Beyond NJ 9842*, pp.53-54
39 Khanna, *Gorichen to Siachen,* p.45
40 Khanna, *Gorichen to Siachen,* p.45
41 Khanna, *Gorichen to Siachen,* p.53
42 Khanna, *Gorichen to Siachen,* pp.50-52
43 Khanna, *Gorichen to Siachen,* p.53
44 Gokhale, *Beyond NJ 9842,* pp.66-67
45 Gokhale, *Beyond NJ 9842,* pp.66-67
46 Gokhale, *Beyond NJ 9842,* pp.66-67
47 *History of Army Air Defence* (New Delhi: Army Air Defence Association, 2008), pp.147-149
48 Gokhale, *Beyond NJ 9842,* pp.67-69
49 Gokhale, *Beyond NJ 9842,* pp.67-69
50 Gokhale, *Beyond NJ 9842,* p.70
51 Gokhale, *Beyond NJ 9842,* pp.70-71
52 Gokhale, *Beyond NJ 9842,* pp.71-72
53 Gokhale, *Beyond NJ 9842,* p.72
54 Gokhale, *Beyond NJ 9842,* p.72
55 Gokhale, *Beyond NJ 9842,* p.72
56 Gokhale, *Beyond NJ 9842,* p.72
57 Gokhale, *Beyond NJ 9842,* pp.73-74
58 Gokhale, *Beyond NJ 9842,* p.74
59 Gokhale, *Beyond NJ 9842,* pp.79-80
60 Gokhale, *Beyond NJ 9842,* pp.79-80
61 Gokhale, *Beyond NJ 9842,* pp.80-81
62 Gokhale, *Beyond NJ 9842,* pp.81-82
63 Gokhale, *Beyond NJ 9842,* p.83
64 Gokhale, *Beyond NJ 9842,* p.83
65 Gokhale, *Beyond NJ 9842,* pp.83-85
66 Gokhale, *Beyond NJ 9842,* p.81-82
67 Gokhale, *Beyond NJ 9842,* p.85
68 Gokhale, *Beyond NJ 9842,* p.87
69 Gokhale, *Beyond NJ 9842,* pp.85-87
70 Gokhale, *Beyond NJ 9842,* pp.85-87
71 Gokhale, *Beyond NJ 9842,* p.89
72 Gokhale, *Beyond NJ 9842,* pp.89-90
73 Gokhale, *Beyond NJ 9842,* p.90
74 Gokhale, *Beyond NJ 9842,* p.90
75 Gokhale, *Beyond NJ 9842,* p.90
76 Gokhale, *Beyond NJ 9842,* p.91
77 Gokhale, *Beyond NJ 9842,* p.91
78 Gokhale, *Beyond NJ 9842,* p.92

Chapter 5

1 Gokhale, *Beyond NJ 9842,* p.99
2 Gokhale, *Beyond NJ 9842,* p.100
3 Gokhale, *Beyond NJ 9842,* p.102
4 Gokhale, *Beyond NJ 9842,* pp.100-101
5 Gokhale, *Beyond NJ 9842,* p.101
6 Gokhale, *Beyond NJ 9842,* pp.101-102
7 Gokhale, *Beyond NJ 9842,* p.103
8 Gokhale, *Beyond NJ 9842,* p.103
9 Gokhale, *Beyond NJ 9842,* p.103
10 Gokhale, *Beyond NJ 9842,* p.103
11 Gokhale, *Beyond NJ 9842,* p.104
12 Gokhale, *Beyond NJ 9842,* p.104
13 Gokhale, *Beyond NJ 9842,* p.106
14 Gokhale, *Beyond NJ 9842,* p.104
15 Gokhale, *Beyond NJ 9842,* p.108
16 Gokhale, *Beyond NJ 9842,* p.108
17 Gokhale, *Beyond NJ 9842,* p.112
18 Gokhale, *Beyond NJ 9842,* p.190
19 Gokhale, *Beyond NJ 9842,* p.191
20 Gokhale, *Beyond NJ 9842,* p.191
21 Gokhale, *Beyond NJ 9842,* p.191
22 Gokhale, *Beyond NJ 9842,* p.192
23 Gokhale, *Beyond NJ 9842,* p.194
24 Gokhale, *Beyond NJ 9842,* pp.195-197
25 Gokhale, *Beyond NJ 9842,* p.199
26 Gokhale, *Beyond NJ 9842,* pp.199-201
27 Gokhale, *Beyond NJ 9842,* pp.201-202
28 J. Hussain, "The Fight for Siachen", *The Tribune,* 22 April 2012
29 Harish Kapadia. *Siachen Glacier: The Battle of Roses* (New Delhi: Rupa Publications Pvt. Ltd. 2010), Kindle edition location 2593-2594
30 Kapadia. *Siachen Glacier*, location 2623-2624

Chapter 6

1 V.P. Malik, *Lessons from Kargil*
2 Gurmeet Kanwal, 'Pakistan's Strategic Blunder at Kargil', *CLAWS Journal*, Summer 2009, pp.55-56
3 Dinesh Kumar, "What it Took and the Run-up to Operation Vijay", *The Times of India,* 19 July 1999.

4 'Saurabh Kalia's parents waging a lone battle to highlight war crimes', *Hindu.com*, 15 June 2012.
5 Kanwal, 'Pakistan's Strategic Blunder at Kargil', p.57
6 Kanwal, 'Pakistan's Strategic Blunder at Kargil', p.57
7 Amarinder Singh, *A Ridge Too Far: War in the Kargil Heights 1999* (Patiala: Motibagh Palace, 2001), pp.42-43
8 Kanwal, 'Pakistan's Strategic Blunder at Kargil', n.1 p.101. A note here – the term JCO means Junior Commissioned Officer and is a rank unique to the armies of India and Pakistan, dating to the British Indian Army. JCOs have no Western equivalent except perhaps, to an extent, Warrant Officers. The very high Officer casualties proportionate to the others reflects a tendency of Indian officers to lead assaults personally even at platoon and section level.
9 Kanwal, 'Pakistan's Strategic Blunder at Kargil' n.1, p.102 & n.65 p.216
10 Pranab Dhal Samanta, 'Musharraf now has Pak's Kargil toll: 357', *Indian Express,* 7 October 2006; 'Ill-Conceived planning by Musharraf led to second major military defeat in Kargil: PML-N', *Pakistan Tribune,* 6 August 2006; 'Pak makes it official, names 453 soldiers killed in Kargil War, *Hinudstan Times,* 18 November 2010
11 Badri-Maharaj, *Kargil 1999*, pp.55-56
12 Badri-Maharaj, *Kargil 1999*, p.48
13 Kapadia, *The Siachen Glacier,* location 2624-2654
14 Gokhale, *Beyond Point NJ 9842,* p.206
15 Gokhale, *Beyond Point NJ 9842,* p.206
16 A. G. Noorani, 'Kargil Diplomacy', *Frontline*, 13 August 1999
17 B. Riedel, 'American Diplomacy and the 1999 Kargil Sumit at Blair House' (University of Pennsylvania: Centre for the Advanced Study of India, 2002), p.5
18 Riedel, p.6
19 Riedel, pp.12-13
20 Khaleeq Kiani, 'Kargil Adventure was a Four-Man Show', *Dawn*, 28 January 2013

Chapter 7

1 Debanish Achom, "Defence Minister Rajnath Singh Bonds With Soldiers At Siachen Over Jalebi", *NDTV,* 3 June 2019
2 Gokhale, *Beyond NJ 9842,* pp.217-218
3 Gokhale, *Beyond NJ 9842,* p.218
4 Gokhale, *Beyond NJ 9842,* p.221-222
5 "Siachen: Pakistan declares buried troops dead after 52 days", AFP, 29 May 2012.
6 Manjeet Negi, "Army provides 1 lakh kit to jawans deployed around Siachen Glacier", *India Today,* 22 January 2020
7 "Indian Army approves 'made-in-India' gear for Siachen troops", *Think Change India,* 21 August 2018 https://yourstory.com/2018/08/indian-army-made-in-india-siachen-troops, and A. Mishra, "Pak army working in deplorable conditions in Siachen", *Sunday Guardian Live,* 14 December 2019
8 Gokhale, *Beyond NJ 9842,* p.154
9 Gokhale, *Beyond NJ 9842,* pp.144-145
10 W.P.S. Sidhu, "Siachen: India and Pakistan continue their war over this desolate landscape", *India Today,* May 31 1992
11 Kunal Verma & Rajiv Williams, *The Long Road to Siachen: The Question Why* (New Delhi: Rupa Publications, 2010), pp.388-390
12 "India and Pakistan start cease-fire in Kashmir", *Reuters,* 26 November 2003
13 S. Aroor & G. Sawant, "Siachen demilitarisation: Could PM gift away to Pakistan what Army has won?", *India Today,* 14 May 2012
14 Aroor & Sawant
15 Iftikhar Gilani, "When MK Narayanan stalled Siachen deal", *DNA India,* 7 September 2017
16 Aroor & Sawant
17 Aroor & Sawant
18 Aroor & Sawant

ABOUT THE AUTHOR

Sanjay Badri-Maharaj, from Trinidad, received is MA and PhD from the Department of War Studies, Kings College London. His thesis was on India's Nuclear Weapons Program. He has written and published extensively, including *The Armageddon Factor: Nuclear Weapons in the India-Pakistan Context* (2000) and *Indian Nuclear Strategy: Confronting the Potential Nuclear Threat from both Pakistan and China* (2018), as well as *Kargil 1999* and *Trinidad 1990* for Helion's @War series. He has served as a consultant to the Ministry of National Security in Trinidad and was a visiting International Fellow at the Institute for Defence Studies and Analyses, New Delhi. This is his third instalment for Helion.